What's Black About It?

OTHER MARKETING BOOKS FROM PMP

The Kids Market: *Myths & Realities*

Marketing to American Latinos, Part I

Marketing to American Latinos, Part II

The Whole Enchilada

Beyond Bogedas: *Developing a Retail Relationship
with Hispanic Customers*

The Mirrored Window: *Focus Groups from a Moderator's Point of View*

The Great Tween Buying Machine

Marketing Insights to Help Your Business Grow

Why People Buy Things They Don't Need

A Knight's Code of Business: *How to Achieve
Character and Competence in the Corporate World*

India Business: *Finding Opportunities in this Big Emerging Market*

Moderating to the Max! *A Full-tilt Guide to Creative
Focus Groups and Insightful Depth Interviews*

Marketing to Leading-Edge Baby Boomers

Clear Eye for Branding: *Straight Talk on
Today's Most Powerful Business Concept*

Advertising to Baby Boomers

What's Black About It? Insights to Increase Your
Share of a Changing African-American Market

Marketing to the New Super Consumer: Mom & Kid

Hispanic Marketing Grows Up:
Exploring Perceptions and Facing Realities

What's Black About It?

Insights to Increase Your Share of a Changing African-American Market

PEPPER MILLER

AND

HERB KEMP

PARAMOUNT MARKET PUBLISHING, INC.

Paramount Market Publishing, Inc.
301 S. Geneva Street, Suite 109
Ithaca, NY 14850
www.paramountbooks.com
Telephone: 607-275-8100; 888-787-8100   Facsimile: 607-275-8101

Publisher: James Madden
Editorial Director: Doris Walsh

Cataloging in Publication Data available
ISBN 0-9725290-9-8

Book design and composition: Paperwork

Contents

3995

115741

Sidebars

Lessons Learned

Acknowledgements

From Pepper Miller

Thank you . . .

God. For every mountain and valley

To the two best men I know. My wonderful husband Ron, who is my very best friend. Thanks for living up to those unconditional six words of love and support: "Don't worry Baby, I've got this." To my dad, John Hunter, the eternal optimist and my hero!

To my children Devonna Hardy and Brandon Miller, and my grandson Jessie Lawrence. I am proud of who you are and your achievements.

To every client who entrusted us with their business. We appreciate the opportunity.

To every respondent who participated in our (and any) research study; Thanks for telling "your truth."

Editors, Jacklynn Topping, our content editor and my good friend; for the endless hours of re-writes, contributions, and thought-provoking assessments; and MJ Rumminger for stepping up to the plate early on.

Bud Mc Cullen, Patricia Lawrence, Pattie Cantella and Danita Ayers; there is no way I could have done any of this without you. I continue to be grateful for an outstanding team!

Linda Cohen—an awesome business coach; Thanks for your contributions and unconditional support.

Reverend Doctor Jeremiah A. Wright, Jr. for your tireless efforts at helping the African-American community learn their story and grow to be "Unashamedly Black and Unapologetically Christian."

Yla Eason, for your wonderful contributions and inspiration.

Herb Kemp, my co-author and great friend. Thanks for the fun. During all the assignments that we have worked on together over the years—from you being in the Client seat, to us working together as partners or colleagues—I have always admired your mind and spirit. You are brilliant and I love your creativity and passion for marketing, and I will always cherish the fun and good times that we have had along the way. Thanks for "keeping it real."

In memory . . . Loretta D. Williams, my best friend and former HMG staffer.

I also dedicate this work . . .

In memory of my mother, RUTH C. HUNTER,
and in appreciation for my mother-in-law,
VIRGIE E. MILLER, who suffers with Alzheimer's disease.

From Herb Kemp

Thank you . . .

Vince Cullers, Barbara Proctor, Byron Lewis, Thomas Burrell, Frank Mingo, Carolyn Jones, and Sam Chisholm, pioneers of ethnic target marketing, for your vision, dedication, and excellence. For sustaining an industry that gave minority advertising professionals an opportunity not just to create ads, but to make a difference in how people of color are seen and how they see themselves.

To my esteemed friends and colleagues in the industry—Larry Aarons, Bernie Drayton, Ted Pettus, Bob Norsworthy, Ron Burns, Peter Schweitzer, and Miriam Muléy for always being there to offer encouragement and a helping hand.

To my wife Dolores for the constant encouragement and emotional support she provided during the many hours it took to complete this book.

To my son, Herbert Kemp III and my daughter, Courtney Kemp-Agboh, who have always made me a proud black father.

Mel Davis of the Michigan Avenue YMCA in Buffalo, New York, a mentor and role model for leveraging my relative talents as a young high school basketball player into an athletic scholarship that allowed me to fulfill my dream of becoming the first member of my family to graduate from college, and the first African American to earn an MBA from the Tuck School of Business at Dartmouth, one of the oldest business schools in the country.

Pepper Miller, my co-author, friend of 25 years, professional colleague, and believer in me. This book would not have been possible without your tireless effort, intellectual stimulation, passion for all things black, and dedication to the insight analysis of the black experience.

In memory . . . Jerry West, my oldest friend and the one who taught me how to drive my first and only stick shift car.

I also dedicate this work . . .

In memory of my mother, ANNA B. KEMP, and my father HERBERT KEMP SENIOR, who are my life role models.

Introduction

Background and Purpose

The idea for *What's Black About It?* originated when African-American marketing executives and experts challenged creative teams to identify the "cultural button" in their communications that would effectively bond Black consumers to a brand, product, service, or idea. We were compelled to write this book to resolve the perpetual conflicts in viewpoint between consumer feedback from our African-American market research interviews, and the messages and products that marketers deliver in the marketplace.

In order to discover *What's Black About It?*—those cultural buttons that fuel effective marketing to African Americans—it is important for marketers to understand:

- The *economic value* of marketing to African Americans.
- The fact that African Americans *have more influence on today's culture and taste* than any other ethnic group in the world.
- The fundamental cultural differences between African Americans and general market consumers that are not addressed through mainstream messages.
- Why mainstream communications may "miss the mark" with African-American consumers.
- How historical and cultural influences shape the perceptions of the African-American consumer.
- Reasons why savvy marketers should reconsider dismissing, or reducing, marketing programs that target this valuable audience.
- The importance of corporate infrastructures that support Black target marketing.

Make no mistake about it; we are not talking about being a "good corporate citizen." This is about maximizing return on investment and increasing market share. It is about "staying in the Black" through a better understanding of the advantages of marketing to African Americans.

To win in the new, more diverse marketplace of the 21st century, marketing to African Americans must become a part of the overall corporate business strategy. This means institutionalizing marketers' knowledge of the Black consumer by replacing assumptions with information, ethnic and social stereotypes with facts and insights, committing to real funding, and establishing a dedicated corporate infrastructure that supports targeted marketing from top to bottom. Only through a better understanding of "what's Black about it?" can marketers feel secure in developing marketing strategies and organizational support that will help them gain their fair share of this large, fast-growing, and influential market.

Who Will Benefit from Reading this Book

The target audience for this book is junior-, middle-, and senior-level marketing and advertising executives in decision-making positions who are currently managing African-American marketing budgets or who are interested in the African-American consumer. Categories include a broad range of new and traditional consumer products and services, including financial services, insurance, telecommunications, technology, retail, food and beverage, packaged goods, travel and leisure, entertainment, fashion, publishing, automotive, health and beauty aids, and pharmaceuticals.

This book is about how to improve the return on marketing (ROM) expenditures though a more insightful understanding and sensitive response to the evolving cultural complexities of the African-American consumer in the 21st century.

Any organization that ignores the importance, evolution, and influence of this projected trillion-dollar market segment may be losing valuable market share to competitors who are committed to increasing top line sales and their narrowing profit margins.

Methodology

What's Black About It? is based on over 30,000 quantitative and qualitative interviews with African Americans, 20 years of market research, more than 20 years of ethnic marketing, and recent thought-provoking interviews with key marketing experts and opinion leaders within the African-American community as well as in the general market.

We selected and interviewed multicultural marketing experts and marketing professionals who have a vested interest in the African-American market. They include marketing executives, scholars, and community influencers.

Additionally, we relied on an extensive variety of secondary research such as books, articles, and government statistics. These resources provide point and counterpoint discussions from a representative sample of marketers and researchers who embrace the African-American market, and those who are not convinced of the segment's value, both in the marketplace, and to their businesses.

Finally, we have used a number of examples to support our findings. Some are descriptions of various strategies and communications developed by certain advertising agencies. The use of these illustrations is not an endorsement of one ad agency, or their work, over another.

Prologue: What is Black?
By Lindy Nelson

It started off like any other day in my job as a language arts resource teacher. Upon arrival at my school, I greeted teachers and began working on my current project. Shortly after the bell, Miss Samuel, another teacher, came over and asked me if I'd come to her class to teach a lesson on color poems.

"No problem," I told her. I smiled to myself because this was one of my favorite lessons. The kids love it, and it really seems to bring out their creativity.

Later that day, I marched confidently into her class bearing my "tools of the trade:" my colorfully lettered chart, my extra pencils, my chalk, my paper, and my already prepared examples of color poems. The lesson began by soliciting color images from the students.

"What things can you think of that are green?" I asked enthusiastically.

"A bluggoe leaf . . . an unripe mango . . . grass . . . skin-ups . . . trees . . . a lunch kit . . . a hair clip . . . an exercise," they responded. I eagerly recorded each and every one of their responses on my chart.

I then shared some examples of color poems (which came from a handout I received from the Ministry). Here are a few examples.

What is Red?

Red is a heart filled with love.
Red is a face when it's angry and mean.
Red is when the door is slammed.
Red is Moses and the burning tree.
Red is a volcano erupting.

LINDY NELSON served as a Peace Corps volunteer in Grenada in the West Indies from 1991 to 1993. This article is reprinted from the *Peace Corps Times*, Number 2, 1993, pp. 32–33, and from *Looking at Ourselves and Others*, available on the Peace Corps website at *www.peacecorps.gov/wws/guides/looking/story31.html*.

What is Black?

Black is the color of hatred.
Black is a gloomy night, ashes,
Tar on the road, a car's tire.
Black is the funeral, dragging slow,
A midnight sound, dark and low.

What is Pink?

Pink is the sky at sunset.
Pink is a kitten's tiny nose.
Pink is the inside of a rabbit's ear.
Pink is how I feel inside on my birthday.
Pink is the joy of being alive.

I then encouraged the children to write a descriptive color poem as a class, with all students offering ideas and suggestions. Hands went up like rockets and children bobbed up and down in their seats, begging to be called on. We composed quite a nice color poem, "What is Blue?" Finally, I put the students into small groups to write their own color poems. They worked well together, cooperating and sharing.

When the lesson was over, I quickly conferred with Miss Samuel to see how she felt about the lesson. We both agreed that the students had made a good effort and have some excellent poems to prove it. I left the class feeling satisfied and went about my duties, without thinking again of the lesson.

The next morning, Miss Samuel came over to have a "piece-a-chat" with me. She told me that something about the lesson I taught had bothered her, but she couldn't put her finger on it at the time. Through-out the evening she thought about it and finally realized it was my example color poem, "What is Black?" She found that my poem used negative images to describe Black and decided to try her hand at presenting Black in a poem with positive images. This is what she came up with.

What is Black?

Black is the shine of ebony
And the color of some people's hair.
Black is the feather of the Corbeau King
And the skin of my ancestors.
Black is the seed of the sweet Sapodilla.
Black is the forerunner of the fair dawn.
Black is Truth.
Black is Justice.
Black is Beautiful.
Black is the writing of Martin Luther King
And the words of Malcolm X.
Black is the philosophy of Marcus Garvey
And the teaching of Bustamante.
Black is the roll of the Tumba drums
And the dancing of the Shango women.
Black is the taste of molasses sweet
And the culture of my people.
Black is the son of King Shaka
And the daughter of Queen Nazinga.
Black is the ring of the Short-Knees' gullo.
Black is Free.
Black is We.
Black is being Me.

As I finished reading her poem, every hair on my body stood on end and tears welled in my eyes. I stammered out some words of praise for her powerful poem and she went on to see about her class.

Unknowingly, Miss Samuel had opened my eyes to my own hidden prejudice. This was upsetting to me because I consider myself extremely open to and accepting of other races and cultures.

I found myself in a Black culture, clearly and unconsciously contributing to negative images associated with Black that have been around for many years. I'm ashamed to admit this and disappointed in myself for this lack of cultural sensitivity.

It started me thinking: Why is it that bad guys always wear Black and good guys wear white? Why do we wear Black for grieving our dead and white to celebrate the joy of the union of marriage? Why is Black associated with death, evil, and hatred while white is associated with angels, purity, and goodness? What kind of message is this sending?

What I know is, I taught the same lesson to nearly every class in my school. Each time, I was unconsciously perpetuating the "negative images" of Black and showing my own "true colors" (excuse the pun). If it wasn't for Miss Samuel, I would have continued my subtle prejudice without even realizing it. So, I owe a lot to her for reminding me, gently, that although we consciously believe in racial equality and unity, sometimes our actions don't show it.

For now, my former example of the color poem "What is Black?" lies at the bottom of my trash bin. I'll be using her powerful images of Black from now on. Thank you, Miss Samuel.

ONE

The Business of Understanding the African-American Market

Sometimes the assumptions we make about others come not from what we have been told or what we have seen on television or in books, but rather from what we have not been told.

—Dr. Beverly Tatum, *Why Are All the Black Kids Sitting Together in the Cafeteria?*

It is amazing that little has been published that discusses the tremendous influence that African Americans have on U.S. popular culture and details specific tactics for marketing to African-American consumers.

With a staggering $761 billion (after tax, disposible income) in annual spending power, projected to exceed $1 trillion by 2010, the African-American market segment is one of the most visible, fastest growing, most influential and yet, most undervalued by consumer group marketers.[1] In December 2004, Robert Coen of Universal McCann projected that U.S. ad spending would be $263.7 billion in 2004. But ad spending that targets African Americans was estimated at barely $1.8 billion by Ken Smikle of *Target Market News*.[2] This translates to less than a 1 percent share (0.68 percent) of total advertising spending.

This paltry investment in African-American marketing suggests that corporate America is not interested in marketing to Blacks in a "Black way"—in self–consciously Black media, using messages calculated to be "culturally relevant" to African-American consumers. We believe that this budget decision is due to inadequate knowledge of the value of marketing to African Americans and the effect on the bottom line.

The Misunderstandings and the Opportunity

Advertising is designed to appeal to different groups. There are
different messages for men, women and children. Why is it not the
same for Blacks, who are not only different by color, but are also
different by culture?
                    —Eugene Morris, CEO, E. Morris Communications Inc.

The new mindset in marketing today focuses on appealing to lifestyle similarities among various demographic segments. Rather than develop relevant communications targeted toward individual groups, the theory is that this "multicultural" approach will appeal to all audiences across the board. Actors and actresses of all ethnic backgrounds now populate today's advertising messages—in virtually every product and service category.

Another new marketing approach is the use of models of indistinguishable or multiracial backgrounds. We believe that this is a good approach—for the general market. Jerome D. Williams, professor of African-American studies at the University of Texas at Austin disagrees with this "new marketing" approach, and says these ads are not representative of how America really lives. "Despite the progress we've made on Civil Rights and other things, if you look at the United States in terms of where we live and who our friends are and where we go to church, we live in different worlds."[3]

This book deals specifically with the African-American market and is not intended to speak to issues among Latinos, Asians, or other minority segments. While similar characteristics, such as age and income, do exist between segments, the blanket assumption that age, lifestyle, and income similarities are more significant than cultural factors among various ethnic groups may be a mistake.

The Miss

The greatest problem in communication is the illusion that it has
been accomplished.
                                        —George Bernard Shaw

In a recent article, author Angela Johnson interviewed Joe Pilotta, VP of Research for BIGresearch, an online market intelligence and internet-powered marketing research firm. According to Ms. Johnson, Pilotta is an advocate for including people of color and their cultural differences in general market advertising. However, he is against developing targeted ads for various consumer groups stating, "There are differences, and some of them are specific, but that divorces them from the dominant culture."[4] Mr. Pilotta strongly believes in focusing on the similarities, despite the documented success of long time major marketers like McDonald's, Coca-Cola, General Motors, who through a greater understanding of the nuances of African-American culture, have created successful, targeted ethnic marketing programs and communications.

Fashion industry experts, for example, now believe that their advertising messages should appeal to people of "diverse racial roots." Lois Huff, vice president of Ohio-based Retail Forward, supports this view, stating, "Lifestyles are expanding across racial lines . . . bodies and budgets tend to change a lot more with age than race."[5]

What Mr. Pilotta, Ms. Huff and the other "new marketers" fail to understand is that the majority of African Americans are "living Black" i.e., living, worshiping, and socializing exclusively with each other, by choice. In fact, diversity for most African Americans, as with most Americans, occurs primarily in the workplace. Otherwise, many African Americans are reading Black newspapers and magazines, visiting Black websites, listening to Black radio (rap, old school, or jazz) and they are seeing billboard-targeted messages primarily in the neighborhoods in which they live. We're not saying that African Americans reject mainstream culture. Rather, it is important for many African Americans to feel connected with each other and to celebrate their unique culture.

Unfortunately, Mr. Pilotta, like many of today's marketers, has missed the point entirely. The lack of relevant, targeted advertising says to African Americans that the way they live life, the way they know life, is not as important as being a member of the so-called "dominant culture."

Ron Franklin, President of NSights Worldwide, LLC of Southfield, Michigan, a full-service strategic market research firm, confirmed this "connection observation" saying during an interview, "The relevance of being African American involves both one's self and one's community."[6]

Staying connected is a means to honor Black culture without pressure from the predominant culture's constant message to "be like us." This is the impetus behind targeted products, programs, and communications that foster the best of Black culture such as Black media, historically Black colleges and universities, Black book clubs, Black churches, Black fraternities and sororities, Black investment clubs, Black children's books . . . well, you get the point.

The idea that targeted efforts separate consumers and "support stereotypes" is a huge misunderstanding. Stereotypes support stereotypes! The key is to target without stereotyping.

The Hit

If you're trying to persuade people to do something, or buy something, it seems to me you should use their language, the language in which they think.

—David Ogilvy, founder, Ogilvy and Mather

The irony in many marketers' misunderstandings about targeted efforts is that, rather than being "divorced from dominant culture" African Americans are, in reality, one of the primary influencers on mainstream culture today.

In other words, if you want the country to become aware of your clothes, listen to your music, and talk your talk, it makes sense to become aware of the importance of the influence of Black culture on mainstream America. It seems suicidal to abandon marketing efforts aimed at the very individuals who are showing the rest of the world how to do it.

When African-American youth start wearing a new style of clothing, the rest of the country soon follows. Hip-hop and rap music is heard blasting from the cars of Asians, Latinos, and white youth every day. As soon as members of the so-called "dominant" culture have overheard another example of African-American slang, they begin using the same phrase in mainstream communications. Witness the *Today Show*'s Katie Couric's repeated use of the phrase "bling-bling" when referencing luxury items.

At the same time, African Americans are unlikely to look to other cultures for cues about clothing, language, music, and behavior. The plain truth is that African Americans are not picking up Asian slang; they are not embracing traditional Indian dress, or listening to heavy metal. Yet, Britney Spears (and countless others) imitates Janet Jackson; the Backstreet Boys sing a sort of pop-R&B using the same video production techniques, and wearing the same type of clothing as Boyz2Men or Usher; Eminem is a white rapper—before him, Vanilla Ice; white guys and girls have dreadlocks. Louis Armstrong, John Coltrane and Duke Ellington were groundbreaking jazz artists long before Tommy Dorsey or Bix Beiderbeck.

Stove Top Recognizes and Embraces African-American Cultural Cues

The following example illustrates the power of words and their interpretation in Black culture.

In the early 1990s, General Foods' Stove Top Stuffing wanted to increase its sales among Black consumers. The company enlisted Burrell Communications, a Chicago-based African-American advertising agency, to create the campaign. Burrell's research revealed that, not only do African Americans use cornbread instead of loaf bread to make their stuffing, but also they refer to stuffing as "dressing."

General Foods developed a cornbread recipe and created a tagline for the African-American market.

Moreover, for many African Americans, use of the word "stuffing" typically referenced the white recipe that called for bread, versus the traditional Black recipe that requires cornbread.

Whereas some whites in the south also use the term "dressing" it is used more commonly among Blacks, and its use is more widespread among African Americans across the country than the regional understanding for whites.

As a result of these findings, Burrell encouraged General Foods to develop a cornbread recipe and they created a tagline for the African-American market that read, "The box says stuffing, but the taste says dressing."[7] Targeted TV radio and print ads were placed in various Black media and Stove Top's awareness, and sales among African Americans, went through the roof.

Multicultural Marketing Misconceptions

Customers buy for their reasons, not yours.
—Orvel Ray Wilson, *Guerrilla Selling*

Multicultural and multiracial marketing are not the same. Multicultural marketing is an indicator that cultural insights are absolutely necessary. *Multiracial* marketing is simply about racial representation—marketers putting different faces into an ad. Unfortunately, what many marketers consider multicultural marketing is, in fact, multiracial marketing. Some examples of advertising and situations that illustrate the multiracial marketing trend include:

- In the 1980s The United Colors of Benetton, a fashion manufacturer and retail chain, created innovative ads that featured extreme close ups of interracial groups of models laughing with each other and hugging.

- Tiger Woods, in the late 1990s, became a champion for the multiracial cause by proclaiming himself "Cablinasian" to embrace his multiracial heritage.

- In 2000 the U.S. Census Bureau extended an invitation to Americans to declare their own specific racial identity, and some people began to identify themselves as biracial or multiracial.

Then, there are the marketing buzzwords—ethnic, multicultural, urban, diversity—endlessly overused by marketers and the general public. While marketers and diversity professionals embrace these expressions, The Reverend Dr. Jeremiah Wright Jr., of Trinity United Church of Christ in Chicago believes the overuse of this language and practice helps create messages that shape erroneous attitudes about the importance of Black culture in particular, and of the Black community's value. "The buzzwords . . . seem to be obvious efforts to exclude relevant cultural nuances that are unique to African Americans. Those words dilute the African experience. They dilute the African reality in our midst. They dilute the unique African-American culture and they dilute the [importance of the African-American] buying power."[8]

As we stated earlier, culture is what makes African Americans respond to messages differently. *Multicultural* marketing is about connecting with the target audience through cultural insights.

Al Anderson, CEO and founder of Anderson Communication Inc., an African-American ad agency based in Atlanta, believes there is *no such thing* as a multicultural person. He says, "Last time I checked, all marketing is targeted at somebody . . . how you construct this young, Black, Latino, Asian person, I don't know. I've never met one of those folks."[9] He also believes that some clients have little connectivity with Black people except for "articulate Blacks"—those who drive BMWs and carry an American Express card. He cautions, "since they don't know anything about Black folk, they then frame their [marketing] decisions based upon their very limited exposure or understanding."[10]

NSights Worldwide's Ron Franklin believes that, "marketers have to communicate personalized needs."[11] He also cautions marketers against ignoring cultural distinctions in favor of a more general message. Rather, marketers should become familiar with the additional cultural needs specific to the African-American consumer—or risk being tuned out entirely by those consumers with the greatest power to influence culture among other market segments.

On some levels, the new "multicultural" strategy appears to be merely a misguided attempt to justify "stretching" marketing dollars in today's lean business environment. It may seem, at first glance, more economically efficient to create a single message that attempts to appeal to all consumers. In fact, this strategy may actually dilute the effectiveness of the campaign among Black consumers specifically, or it may backfire entirely.

While the "multiracial" approach may not be wrong, *per se,* the assumption that Black consumers will respond to general (mass) market communications has been proven false in several research studies. The positive financial outcomes for those companies that invest in targeted programs also supports the case for targeted marketing. These studies and programs, discussed later in this book, found that African Americans continue to be more responsive to communications and programs that speak directly to them in a positive and culturally relevant manner. And they are also more attentive to models or spokespersons who look like them.

What's in a Name?

"Black" or "African American" racial labels make little difference in how African Americans want to be addressed.

In 1993, The Roper Organization conducted a survey among African Americans to determine preference on how they want to be addressed. At that time, only 30 percent of Blacks preferred the term "African-American," 42 percent preferred Black, 10 percent preferred Afro-American, and 18 percent preferred some other term or didn't know.

African American or Black?

In 2001, the Gallup Newswire found that many sources indicate that 40 to 45 percent of African Americans say they had no preference between the terms "Black" or "African American."

However, when asked what they preferred being called on a personal level, Blacks typically show a slight preference for the term "Black" over "African American." On the other hand, when asked what they preferred the race to be called, a majority of Blacks said they preferred the term "African American" over "Black."

This finding is in sync with The Hunter-Miller Group's qualitative findings with African Americans across the country. We learned that when many African Americans use the term "Black" with each other, it is associated with intimacy and familiarity. However, when the race is referenced publicly or formally by both African Americans and non-African Americans, many prefer the term "African American."

TWO

A Business Case for Marketing to African Americans

You must have mindshare before you can have market share.
—Christopher M. Knight, author and internet strategist

The Numbers Don't Lie

Today whether you are an established market leader looking for new markets, or a newcomer to ethnic marketing who thrives on new ideas, African-American consumers represent a major business opportunity.

African Americans have the capability and desire to purchase. African-American buying power has increased 127 percent since 1990, to $761 billion in 2005. This buying power is projected to increase 33 percent to $965 billion by 2009, notably outpacing buying power growth for the general population. This market consists of younger, geographically concentrated, urban consumers who are realizing significant gains in terms of socioeconomic status due to improving educational status and entrepreneurial pursuits. These consumers are socially conscious and prefer supporting diversity friendly companies and stores.

In many product categories, ranging from automobiles to packaged goods, the African-American propensity for buying branded, high-ticket and high-margin items makes them more loyal and profitable customers than any other consumer segment. With improving socioeconomic status, African Americans represent a major untapped customer acquisition opportunity for many new and emerging product and service categories, particularly in the areas of financial services, travel, internet, insurance, and pharmaceutical products. Further, African Americans are avid users of various media and are responsive to targeted initiatives that address their lifestyles and beliefs. In fact, from 1999 to 2003 there were 57 new magazine launches targeting African Americans representing a mix of categories and interests including business and travel, parenting, religion, and automotive.[12]

Equally important, African Americans have been, and continue to be, one of the primary trendsetter segments among general and ethnic markets—especially in the realms of music, fashion, sports, and language. Marketers who consciously establish a relationship with this lucrative yet still underserved market, by better understanding the African-American mindset, attitudes, behavior, and lifestyle, will reap significant long-term rewards from a loyal, influential customer base.

The Power of African-American Spending [13]

African-American spending is evident across many categories including:

Hair Care: African Americans account for more than 30 percent of this $4 billion industry.

Automobiles: 63 percent of African-American households own a vehicle that was purchased used, and 37 percent own a vehicle that was purchased new according to the Selig Center of Economic Growth.

Telephone Service: Expenditures in this category total $918 per person annually or 8.1 percent more than the national average.

Personal Clothing: According to a 2001 study by Cotton Incorporated, African Americans spent an average of $1,427 on clothing per year for themselves, $458 more than the average consumer.

> African Americans spend more per year on clothing for themselves than average consumers.

Electronics: Nearly twice as many African Americans (60 percent vs. 32 percent) spend money on TVs, radios and sound equipment.

Food: African-American families spend 30 percent more on weekly groceries than the U.S. average at large, according to Kraft Foods.

Travel: Travel volume among African Americans increased 4 percent between 2002 and 2003, considerably higher than the 2 percent growth in U.S. travel overall during the same period.[14]

Finance: The goals for spending, saving and investing differ between Blacks and whites:[15]

	BLACKS	WHITES
Education spending	38%	23%
Saving for children's education	20%	14%
Retirement	44%	58%

They Speak English, Don't They?

Black folks are not dark-skinned white people.
—Tom Burrell, Founder and CEO Emeritus,
Burrell Communications

The growth of other ethnic markets, particularly the Spanish-speaking market, has also given rise to some complacency about marketing to Blacks. The current prevailing notion with regard to Blacks is basically, "They speak English, don't they?" assuming that African Americans will respond to any message simply because it's spoken in English. It is this rhetorical question, combined with the mistaken assumption underlying it, that is the foundation for the creation of non-productive, marketing efforts in which the messages are assumed to be as effective among Blacks as they are to the general market.

The absence of a language barrier has become a major rationalization for reduced spending, generic messaging, and inadequate market research when targeting African Americans. Today, many marketers give only a nod to this segment and its $761 billion annual spending power. In many cases, the African-American market is simply not on the radar.

While many marketers are increasingly aware of these facts, and the size and vitality of the African-American market, they often fail to take the best advantage of it. The lack of a deep and relevant understanding of the Black consumer results in inadequate spending and overestimation of the ability of general-market strategies to effectively reach African Americans. Some marketers use the "language issue" to rationalize blending African-American budgets with general-market plans while spending more on the Latino segment. Or they may buy media directed toward African Americans, but their message does not speak effectively to this target.

In defense of some marketers, we do understand their conundrum. Many are forced to make choices from a business situation that looks like this:

I have a budget of "X" dollars.

My general market budget is "Y" and,

I have "Z" dollars to reach other ethnic segments.

The outcome from the above is that, in many cases, African-American marketing is rolled in with the general market. Marketers are under pressure to boost market share and improve return on investment (ROI), in part by spending less on marketing. As a result, today's marketing executives may adopt erroneous notions about how to market to African Americans that underestimate the value of the African-American consumer and ultimately lead to ineffective marketing messages.

The futility of this approach is best illustrated through the use of a metaphor:

> Imagine a commercial fisherman who wants to catch a specific type of fish (zFish) because it is popular, valuable and, best of all, zFish are pretty much the leader of the pack among other fish—where you find zFish, other valuable fish aren't far away.
>
> This fisherman doesn't really know much about zFish; he never saw any when he was growing up, he hasn't seen many of them in his adult life, and he knows very little about their habitat, or their lifecycle. He doesn't know whether it's better to catch them in a gill net, a purse seine net, or with a rod and reel.
>
> He's not rich, so he's operating with a limited budget.
>
> Since he's been a fisherman his whole life he decides he can't afford to spend a lot of time or money trying to find out about catching zFish. He's caught a lot of fish with nets before.
>
> He decides to build a huge net to scoop up all the fish and then hopes he catches zFish in the process. Yeah, it should work. After all, fish are fish . . . right?

Well, it's one strategy.

However, if zFish live at 600 feet below the surface and he's trolling at 300 feet, it's unlikely that he'll catch very many zFish. If zFish live in the Pacific Ocean and he's fishing in the Atlantic . . . or if they run at dusk and he goes out at dawn every day to catch them, he may indeed catch some fish, but it's likely the elusive zFish will remain out of reach.

In today's tough business environment, marketers must understand the value of the African-American market as both influencers and consumers, and target their messages to that audience. Only then will they be able to maximize their bottom line, and put their companies at a competitive advantage moving into the future.

THREE

Where African Americans Lead, the World Follows

How is it that you can disrespect a man's ethnicity when you know we have influenced every facet of white America, from our music, style of dress, not to mention your basic imitation of our sense of cool, walk, talk, dress, mannerisms. We enrich your very existence, all the while contributing to the gross national product through our achievements in corporate America.

—Sin Russell, portrayed by Cedric the Entertainer
in the movie, *Be Cool*

The African-American market is not only one of the largest and fastest growing segments, but African Americans possess the extraordinary added value of influencing the consumer purchasing decisions of the rest of America *and the world*. Susan Mboya, head of P&G's new multicultural business development unit, states, "What Black folks buy, particularly what young Black consumers buy, everybody will buy afterward."[16]

Author Leon E. Wynter illuminates the influence and contributions within specific categories and among certain firms. "Anheuser-Busch in beer, Philip Morris in cigarettes, Coke in soft drinks, Smirnoff in spirits, and McDonald's in fast food have long recognized the competitive edge to be gained through crucial share points, and fractions of share points, in a cutthroat marketplace by targeting African Americans—or to be lost by allowing a competitor to beat them to it."[17] Among other companies that have more recently followed this lead are Avon, KFC, Ford, Revlon, Cover Girl, and Tommy Hilfiger, to mention just a few.

Additionally, Byron Lewis, Chairman and CEO of Uniworld Group, an African-American advertising firm, speaks about marketers' embrace of African-American influence, and at the same time, their avoidance of African-American consumers: "But the truth is that [the term] 'urban' is used to avoid giving prominence to urban's source—the Black experience. It is the Black consumer who is the engine. Jazz, rhythm and blues, rap, hip-hop, this is the influence."[18]

Early Adopters

African Americans are more likely than whites to be among the first to set new trends, and to consider themselves on the cutting edge:

- 34 percent are likely to keep up with changes in trends and fashions (compared with 25 percent of whites).[19]
- 20 percent of African Americans vs. 7 percent of whites use wireless telephone service, 46 percent vs. 18 percent of whites use data input.
- 71 percent of African Americans vs. 65 percent of whites say it is important to keep up with the latest technology products and services.[20]
- 48 percent say they *need* to keep up on the latest trends in movies, music and TV. [21]
- Jeff Meade, business development manager for The Rebel Organization, a company that connects brands to the street, describes the influencer process from innovator to mass market as follows: "Innovators embrace products out of necessity. Nelly, for example, may use a Sidekick because it allows him to be in touch with people all the time without talking to them. Trendsetters (Black youth) see Nelly pick up the product and introduce it to their peers. Marketers need trendsetters to pick it up. The mass needs trendsetters to validate the product."

> African Americans want to stay on the cutting edge.

Black Influence Turns the Corner

The ability to generate significant influence beyond its own market segment is a truly unique quality of African Americans. No other segment comes close to exerting the influence on fashion, music, slang, sports and the overall perception of what is cool around the world than African Americans.

Every year, ad agencies commit millions of dollars on behalf of their clients to the largest advertising blitz in the country—Super Bowl Sunday. The Super Bowl broadcast is the most visible, most expensive media buy in the world. The commercials are the most anticipated on a global level. Creative ideas and production quality has to be outstanding. It's the one television program in which the commercial breaks capture and hold audience attention as much as, or more than, third down and inches with eight seconds left at the end of the second half.

The commercials seen during the Super Bowl define and reflect the mindset and cultural face of America. Advertisers in the 2005 Super Bowl spent a record $2.4 million per 30-second spot.[22] Interestingly, African-American celebrities, icons, music, and talent drove many of the big money commercials:

- **Pepsi**: Sean "Puffy" Combs—in this spot, Combs gets to an awards show by hitching a ride in a Diet Pepsi truck. Other celebrities, including Carson Daly, mistake the truck for P. Diddy's stylish new wheels and rush out to buy Diet Pepsi trucks of their own. (Ironically, this ad reinforces the powerful premise of this book—that African Americans are trendsetters and what African Americans do, everyone else imitates.)

- **Anheuser-Busch**: two spots featuring Cedric the Entertainer.

- **Frito-Lay**: MC Hammer

- **Nationwide Financial Services**: MC Hammer

- **MBNA**: Gladys Knight plays rugby for the credit card–issuer

- **Silestone:** Dennis Rodman is featured in a bathtub for the counter-top company

- **Sony Pictures**: Will Smith stars in the film comedy *Hitch*

- **Pepsi**: iTune promotion giveaway stars Eve and Gwen Stefani

The companies listed above, along with several others, illustrate the rewards of transcending the color barrier by using African-American celebrities as part of their marketing strategy. They own a lion's share of the lucrative and loyal African-American market, and lots of other segments want to be influenced by them.

Who could ask for more?

FOUR

Illuminating the Black Experience

For the past 20 years, The Hunter-Miller Group has conducted strategic research on the African-American market. During this time, we have uncovered several critical insights about the way African Americans view themselves, how they conduct their lives, and how they interact with various forms of marketing communications.

These insights, which describe the Black experience in terms of identity, lifestyle, and interaction with communications and media, are outlined in this and the following chapters and serve as the foundation for much of the information presented in this book. We invite you to take a view through our lens, imagine how to employ these insights, and learn how to talk and market effectively to African Americans.

A Glimpse into the Black Experience

We are positively a unique people. Breathtaking people. Anything we do, we do big! Despite attempts to stereotype us, we are a crazy, individual, and an uncorrallable people.
　　　　　　　　—Leontyne Price, soprano, Metropolitan Opera (retired)

There is no single Black experience. Age, education, economics, geography, lifestyle, mindset, family and community cultures—even skin color—are some of the primary characteristics that affect how one Black person's experience in America might be similar to, or different than, another person's Black experience. Given the vast number of theories and books written on the subject, we can only hope to provide a partial view about the Black experience within the scope of this book. We will try, however, to provide a framework with which to support the insights that we have learned about the African-American market over the years.

The Melting Pot Myth

I know that America is becoming a melting pot of different people and cultures, and that's ok. But why do they all have to melt white?
—Jacklynn Topping, Black writer and business strategist,
to a white colleague who did not understand her need
to stay connected to Black culture

One misconception held by many marketers is the assumption that African Americans want to (or should) abandon their culture for the predominant white culture. It is true that African Americans have a strong desire to be acknowledged, respected, and to feel included in the American culture. However, an important aspect of the Black Experience for most African Americans is to "keep it real"—to stay close to their roots, connected to their culture, heritage and people.

Henry Louis Gates' book and BBC–PBS documentary *America Behind the Color Line* provides an exposé of the Black experience by gauging the economic, political, and social progress that African Americans have made since the death of Dr. Martin Luther King, Jr. After conducting several interviews within different segments of the African-American population across the country, one of Gates' key findings was how important Black culture was to most of the participants, especially among the middle class subjects he interviewed. "Perhaps the two biggest surprises—certainly to me—about the collective behavior of the members of the Black middle class are, first, their deep and abiding embrace of Black culture, and of a Black cultural nationalist social identity and second, the desire of many to live in their own neighborhoods with other Black middle class."[23]

When African Americans are asked to provide past and present depictions of the Black experience, Baby Boomers are more likely to reference the Civil Rights era as a memorable and significant period in their lives. Boomers often mention the importance of maintaining, or salvaging Black culture. The Reverend Doctor Jeremiah A. Wright, Jr., points to his recollection of past experiences as a "mixed" time of joy and terror. He also reveals that at one time, the urban Black community was more united through the Black church and cites integration as a reason for some loss of that unity. "The Black experience was primarily centered around the church and the activities that took place in the Black community. We moved into integrated neighborhoods and we lost the bonding we once had in the Black community."[24]

Jill Nelson, best-selling author of fiction and non-fiction from an African-American perspective, echoes Dr. Wright's sentiments, "Segregation forced more similar experiences. We had a Black community . . . it does not serve our interest to not have a community."[25]

On the other hand, the hip-hop culture is more top of mind with GenXers and youth when sharing their point of view about the Black experience. Darius Howard, a GenX executive at Guerrilla Tactics Media (GTM), an award winning multicultural experiential marketing and communications firm, sees hip-hop and its neo-wealth persona as the catalyst that united Black people and moved them forward. "We didn't have a Black culture unit until hip-hop came along; it unified the people. It gave us something . . . wealth, opportunity, music, fashion. It was our voice."[26]

Although Boomers and GenXers identify with different aspects of the Black experience, they tend to agree that Black culture, values, and community are important characteristics of the survival of the Black community.

The Filter©

Every day of my life, I walk with the idea I am Black, no matter how successful I am.
                                                    —Danny Glover, actor and activist

Dr. Na'im Akbar one of the world's preeminent African-American psychologists and a pioneer in the development of an African-centered

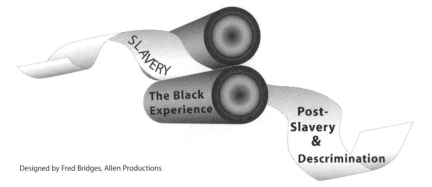

Designed by Fred Bridges, Allen Productions

approach in modern psychology, reminds us that African Americans maintain one very distinguishable characteristic from any other U.S. cultural or racial group—the psychological baggage from slavery, post slavery, and discrimination. We identify this distinctive catalytic outlook as *The Filter*.

The Filter is the nucleus of the Black experience and Black culture. It is a common bond among all African Americans that has had an astounding impact on how others see African Americans, and on how they see themselves, in every aspect of their lives. *The Filter* has predisposed many African Americans to become overly sensitive about feeling stereotyped and not feeling valued, respected, included, and welcomed. It also explains why many African Americans want to be seen as a heterogeneous rather than homogeneous group, to desire real inclusion, to see more and see differently when it comes to marketing communications, to rely upon word-of-mouth, to use general market media, but embrace Black media, to have a high propensity for instant gratification, and be more apt to use kairos time. As a result, many African Americans care about how they are represented, and how white Americans perceive them.

Our interpretation of Danny Glover's comment above is not meant to indicate that he lacks value about himself or his accomplishments. It does however remind us of how the impact of *The Filter* can often foster a mindset that is either "less than" among most African-American and non-African-American consumers, or at least "different than" or "apart from" most African Americans.

The "No Diss" Factor or, Respect and the Black Experience

The status of African Americans has improved on many fronts. Empowered by both formal education and "street smarts," Blacks continue to advance through educational attainment that, in turn, significantly influences societal roles, socioeconomic status and purchasing power in consumer markets. However, one of the fundamental outcomes of *The Filter* is the African Americans' strong desire and need for respect that spans all generations because, after all these years, many African Americans still do not believe they are respected by society at large.

Although this mindset is more apparent among Civil Rights era Boomers, it is also evident across all segments of the African-American population. Additionally, even though most of the youth today are more comfortable with race than were previous generations, one of the primary differences between Black and white youth is that Black youth do not feel that they are as equally respected as white youth.

Over the years, there have been numerous research examples that further express the sentiments of African-American consumers.

- When Yankelovich asked African Americans and whites in 1995 to list and rank deciding factors on where to shop, both agreed that price was number one. However, the second most important factor for whites was the availability of merchandise, while for African Americans, it was respect from retail employees. In fact, 10 years later, the 2005 Burrell Communications–Yankelovich *Multicultural Monitor*, reports that 46 percent of Blacks (vs. 35 percent of whites) feel unwelcome in a store.[27]

- We conducted a variety of focus groups and quantitative research studies with African Americans between 2002 and 2004 for several Fortune 500 insurance companies, local and national banks, major airlines, and mass retailers. As part of the research, African Americans shared their experiences when interacting with these businesses. When discussing customer service, "lack of respect" surfaced prominently, and was described as poor treatment from sales and customer service personnel and blatant disrespect.

- Further, in the Gallup Poll's *2003 Race Relations* survey, nearly half of all African Americans surveyed (49 percent) reported that they had experienced at least one incident of discrimination during the previous 30 days, in settings ranging from stores (26 percent), to restaurants and theaters (18 percent) to public transportation (10 percent).

Marketing professionals (Black, white and others) who develop and promote stereotypical messages and programming may inadvertently arouse these sensitivities. Thus, marketers, particularly those in retail, need to be aware that many African Americans, when confronted with these situations believe, "this (unacceptable treatment) is happening to me because I'm Black."

Of course, anyone could easily draw the same conclusion when they receive disrespectful treatment. They may wonder for example, "Is this happening to me because I'm old, not well dressed, fat, or because I'm white?" Because of the affect of *The Filter,* many African Americans expect to be discriminated against, and unfortunately, some look for it. Without respect, African Americans don't feel welcome in any environment whether a department store, bank or other service office in, or outside, their community.

Protective Radar:© For Members Only

African Americans possess a Protective Radar mindset that is driven by the desire to conduct themselves in such as way as to publicly avoid reinforcing negative stereotypes. The opinion of society matters. For many African Americans, this is a wholly pervasive aspect of life, with much at stake.

There are two different behaviors that stem from the Protective Radar mindset. First, there are certain situations, stories, and expressions that many African Americans feel should be shared only among the African-American community. This could be in the form of a joke, constructive criticism, or any situation or activity that, when exposed outside the boundaries of the Black community, could be viewed as stereotypical.

For example, during his address at an NAACP event in 2004, Bill Cosby pointed the finger at low-income African Americans, charging them with poor parenting skills. When a white reporter quoted him in the *Washington Post,* the African-American community went up in arms —against Mr. Cosby. He was accused of airing the Black community's "dirty laundry" and became an instant enemy of sorts to that community. His good-guy philanthropist image was irrelevant because of this perceived betrayal, although Cosby and his wife Camille have given millions of dollars to Historically Black Colleges and Universities. Other African Americans saw Mr. Cosby's remarks as a type of "victim blaming" or attacking the less unfortunate. Still others were concerned that, because of the publicity, white conservatives would use the statements to reinforce existing negative stereotypes about Blacks and especially poor Blacks.

Ellis Cose, an African-American editor wrote a story in *Newsweek* about this incident and obtained comments and feedback from the segment (poor, primarily urban, single Black parents) that Cosby criticized. However, response from the white community was limited to journalists reporting the story in smaller publications than *Newsweek*, and offered very little, if any, commentary or criticism.[28]

The second manifestation of Protective Radar is the desire for unconditional respect for African-American heroes and public figures. One recently publicized example was the Black community's reaction to the popular *Barber Shop* movies, directed by rapper-turned-producer-director, Ice Cube. A joke in the original movie that angered some African Americans, primarily Baby Boomers, centered around Rosa Parks who, in 1956, ignited the Civil Rights Movement when she refused to give her seat to a white passenger on a bus in Montgomery, Alabama. Actor/comic Cedric the Entertainer's character cracked the infamous joke, "Rosa Parks didn't want to give up her seat because she was tired." It left many African Americans feeling that the movie disrespected an African-American heroine, disrespected the Civil Rights Movement and fostered stereotypes about African Americans in general.

As with the Cosby incident, while there may have been some sympathetic stories from white journalists here and there, there is little evidence that white Americans were offended by the remark, or even viewed it in a negative way. In fact, satirical programs like *Saturday Night Live* and *Mad TV* often make fun of popular white celebrities, icons and leaders without igniting any anger from the white community and these parodies are certainly not perceived as hurting the entire white race.

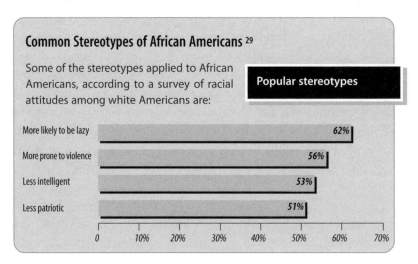

Common Stereotypes of African Americans [29]

Some of the stereotypes applied to African Americans, according to a survey of racial attitudes among white Americans are:

Popular stereotypes

More likely to be lazy	62%
More prone to violence	56%
Less intelligent	53%
Less patriotic	51%

0   10%   20%   30%   40%   50%   60%   70%

Perhaps marketers can better understand the relevance of this when they realize how prevalent stereotyping still is toward Blacks (and other ethnic groups). Regardless of the general belief among whites that this is a multicultural society, it has not eliminated the disparity in how Blacks and whites feel about equality. It follows logically that African Americans feel a need to be portrayed in positive ways and they will appreciate those who do so. This creates an open invitation and an opportunity for marketers.

The Mask

African Americans feel a general need to present a different image of themselves to the public than the image they share when among other African Americans. When questioned about this behavior in focus groups, many admit to having a "Black face" and a "white face." Simply put, when talking to whites, many African Americans believe that, in order to counteract any negative or erroneous stereotypes related to African Americans, they often use language and accents that seem and sound "less Black"—i.e., more white. They are keenly aware that people outside the Black community may view their different speech patterns and language negatively.

Conversely, there is also a tendency by most African Americans to use familiar slang, cultural references, and expressions within the community, around friends, or at home. This is used to establish rapport or affinity and it creates a level of comfort.

The Mask, this "double consciousness," is probably the most ubiquitous—but also one of the most misunderstood—aspects of the Black experience.

Actress Natalie Portman, 23, was quoted in the August 2004 issue of *Allure* magazine after having read W.E.B Dubois' *Souls of Black Folk*. She said, "I'm not Black, but I know what it feels like" unintentionally igniting anger among African Americans. The Harvard graduate who later wrote a letter of apology to *Allure* explained that she could never know what it is like to live life as a Black person, "rather I know what Dubois' concept of double-consciousness feels like."[30]

LESSONS LEARNED ▼

Avoid Ebonics

Ebonics is a colloquial speech many African Americans use, almost exclusively, with each other. In an attempt to relate to the Black community, marketers may try to utilize Ebonic jargon in an effort to establish a commonality—i.e., "speaking the language." More often than not, this strategy will be perceived as off the mark and insulting, and will probably backfire.

A recent McDonald's banner that ran on *ESPN.com* pictured a young man thinking, "Double cheeseburger? I'd hit it." Apparently the creators of this ad did not realize that "hit it" is slang for having sex. Blogger Andrew Teman said, "I firmly believe that McDonald's is not advocating hot *man-on-sandwich* action, but it is quite obvious that they did not do their homework on urban slang."[31]

Amen.

Don't confuse dialects or accents with Ebonics

African Americans have as many differences in their speech patterns as any other Americans. For example, Blacks from the south, speak differently than those who live in New York City. West Indians will speak differently than Blacks in Detroit. Many African Americans don't even speak Ebonics, nor do they speak with a so-called "Black" accent or pronunciation. Some African Americans don't like Ebonics or other stereotypical jargon, believing that it "sounds ignorant" and reinforces a negative stereotype.

Don't use "Black talk"

Most importantly, many African Americans are deeply offended when spoken to by a white person who's trying to "talk Black"—by mimicking mannerisms or slang—and many resent the implication that all Blacks speak in Ebonics.

The Badge

African Americans have identity-shaping relationships with brands. Particular upscale, top-end brands are visible symbols of success for communicating social and economic achievements. To many African Americans, premium brand names are mechanisms that facilitate the buying process. They are a reflection of aspirations in that they provide conspicuous "badges" of social status—a means for eliminating stereotypes, fulfilling emotional needs, and staying on top of the latest trends. Because of the effects of The Filter, the use or display of upscale brands confers upscale status to African-American consumers.

African Americans have a strong sense of pride in their appearance, combined with the belief that they can determine the best look for themselves. Pamela Macklin, former fashion director at *Essence* magazine said it best, "You could safely say that in the African-American culture, being an individual—having a piece of clothing that is different—is a big part of forming one's identity. It is also a culture that tends to be more label-conscious and loyal to those brands."[32]

Badge Value

Overall, when compared with whites, African Americans place a greater emphasis on brand names:[33]

- Brand name is important in all product categories, including food; Blacks prefer national name brands and are less likely to buy private label or generics.

- Blacks were more than twice as likely as whites (30 percent versus 14 percent) to indicate that brands let others know where they are on the social ladder. It is important to have "badge" items to show others they have made it.

- 76 percent of Blacks versus 63 percent of whites said brands represent their unique tastes and individuality.

- Black women are nearly twice as likely as white women to say brands reflect who they are.

- 70 percent of Blacks claimed brand names make it easier and quicker for them to purchase items, which means that brand is a form of quality control that minimizes purchasing risks.

- 58 percent of Blacks compared with 49 percent of whites, stated that brands give them a level of emotional satisfaction.

- 54 percent of Blacks, versus 38 percent of whites, said brand names keep them informed about what's new and trendy.

When African Americans were asked how they defined the best brands, "advertised brands" rated more highly than "performance." However, if the brand does not live up to its promise, it will be rejected.

Of course a brand name is not the only factor that influences purchasing decisions and loyalty. Socioeconomic status and other factors may influence African Americans' responses to specific brands. Black

Connect with African-American Sensibilities

• If you are not targeting African Americans today, extend an invitation to patronize your brand or business.

• Uplift the African-American community every chance you get!

Spike DDB helps State Farm connect with African-American savers

Spike DDB (Spike), an African-American ad agency, understood that African Americans had different reasons for saving and investing than white consumers. So, when its client, State Farm, expressed interest in wooing African Americans toward State Farm's financial services products in addition to insurance, Spike was ready with a rationale and a strategy.

Using statistics to demonstrate that saving for education was a priority for African Americans (vs. saving for retirement which is more important to whites) Spike created a print campaign that featured a child on a bed with outstretched arms, standing in front of a mostly exposed Morehouse banner on the wall and wearing an oversized sweatshirt from Morehouse College. The headline and sub-headlines read, "The only thing that will grow faster is the cost of a college education." And the first line of the body copy reads, "Kids grow up fast, and soon it's time for college."

Prior to rollout, when tested in qualitative research, this message was very compelling and arresting for African-American respondents. Reginald Osborne, Account Director for Spike explains, "For African Americans, education is an important key to success and improving their consumers consider not only the brand name but also how it speaks to them. Black respondents said they are more likely to support a brand that is marketing to them directly and giving back to their community. When speaking to this audience, it's important to get beyond the obvious and understand the reasons for loyalty to certain brands.[34]

There are also affordable categories among the larger masses of African Americans that carry badge value yet don't necessarily require a "fit" with the desirable African-American middle class' economic profile. This outlay is the delivery of pleasure that personalizes, or represents, worth i.e., the value is bigger than what they have to pay. Some

quality of life so that they can save for retirement. African Americans feel very proud when we see our sons and daughters achieving various levels of education at the college or graduate level." Osborne further explains the importance of the Morehouse symbolism. "Historically Black Colleges and Universities (HBCUs) are an important cultural cue for African Americans and Morehouse, is looked upon as the Harvard of the Black community." The campaign ran for over two years from 2002 through 2005 and it, along with another print ad, successfully accomplished State Farm's goals, which were to increase awareness of State Farm's financial services among African Americans.

Promote under-provided positive images
Culturally sensitive, positive, and relevant appeals that celebrate the culture rather than reinforce stereotypes continue to be elements that are more likely to gain the attention and loyalty of African Americans. Therefore, develop strategies and communications that reverse the common stereotypes by including:

- Upscale African-American individuals and families
- African-American family units (including the Black father as an emotionally engaged and responsible caretaker)
- African Americans working with and helping other African Americans
- African-American women in integrated leadership roles
- African-American men in integrated leadership roles (very important)
- African Americans involved in technology and health care

of these categories that over-deliver against the African-America target
and provide status value or a personal connection with their peers are:

- *Fast food*— McDonald's: "MickeyD"
- *Cigarettes*—Kool was "cool"
- *Liquor*—Hennessey: "Henny", Seagram's Gin: "Bumpy Face"
- *Soft drinks*—Coke and Pepsi have status value
- *Sportswear*— Nike and Adidas have status value
- *Electronics*— Sony has status value

Additionally, although $150 for athletic shoes may seem expensive
to some, as a status symbol, the badge-value emotion can be experienced without having to buy an expensive house or luxury car.

Kairos Time

Blacks have a different relationship with time. The use of time in African
culture is driven by kairos time (meaning, as it comes up) and the characteristic African-American need for instant gratification vs. being clock
or calendar driven. Additionally, economic and social circumstances
often have a high degree of impact on the African-American community, which forces them to live day-to-day and use both chronological
and kairos time in their daily lives. This cultural and situational custom
is observed by many African Americans and is an important insight for
marketers to consider, particularly when planning events targeting this
segment.

Separate but related, a common saying in the African-American community, when describing the apparent disregard for their own punctu-
ality and to distinguish Black folks' timing vs. white folks' timing, is the
phrase, "CP Time" (Colored People's Time). Most likely an offshoot
from kairos time theory, "CP Time" is an inside joke within the community but is an unwanted stereotype when viewed from outside the
community.

LESSONS LEARNED ▼

Scheduling Promotions on "Kairos" Time

Advertising and promoting an event too far in advance often leaves room for African Americans to forget or make another choice. When planning events for the African-American market, and depending on the event, plans should be evaluated closely to consider the kairos element, i.e., how far in advance or close to the date of the event should the schedule run. For example, in 2002, the Chicago Symphony Orchestra (CSO) received a two-year grant from the Joyce Foundation to reach out to underserved minority communities. The Symphony began its outreach program to the African-American community—Classical Tapestry—and, aided by research conducted by HMG, targeted key concerts to the African-American market.

The CSO's typical marketing plan includes a direct mail schedule that begins in May for a September opening. Given that African Americans tend to live day-to-day with less interest in the distant future, HMG recommended that direct mail and advertising be implemented closer to the opening night concert date. In addition to releasing its message closer to the concert dates, the CSO reserved a number of tickets for last-minute purchasers.

This proved to be successful for the CSO as the targeted and thoughtfully planned advertising made the concerts more top-of-mind for the Black audience. The CSO has taken this kairos time characteristic into consideration and incorporated it into its subsequent African-American marketing plans. In addition to other efforts, this understanding was one of the elements that helped the CSO build a relationship with a new market segment.

FIVE

Shades of Blackness

The application of segmentation is so important for marketing to the African-American consumer because companies need to align their brands with the sub-segments of this population that will provide them with the best ROI. In order to return the best ROI, it is important to evaluate sub-segments based on who they are, where they live, what touch points are important to them and the brand experience.
—Verdia Johnson, President, Footsteps Advertising

Most African Americans are, and want to be viewed as, heterogeneous rather than homogeneous. Like any other ethnic group, African-American opinions differ based on age, gender, socioeconomic status, education, and cultural mindset. Black people may be conservative or liberal; religious or not; city dwellers or rural residents; educated or not; fair-skinned or brown; low-income or wealthy, or everything in between. These differences may be tied to geographic, family, or educational influences. Yet, African Americans are still tied together by their common history and culture. That commonality is the inextricable bond (The Filter) that makes the segment unique.

Despite the great significance "the differences" make in a campaign that successfully markets to African Americans, such differences are often unknown to marketers. Ten years ago, Yankelovich's *African-American Monitor* included an African-American segmentation study and identified three key segments: GenXers, Boomers, and Matures.

GenXers	Boomers	Matures
Born 1965–1984	Born 1940–1964	Born 1925–1939

Today, marketers and researchers generally identify and reference GenXers, Boomers, and Matures within all consumer segments. These three key segments reference specific age groups and certain similar characteristics that influence behavior and preferences. Understanding how, where, and why African Americans fall into these different segments is critical for developing relevant and effective "talking to me" marketing plans and communications.

While it's not the intention of this book to outline every segment of the African-American population, this chapter will attempt to further clarify certain characteristics of African-American GenXers, Boomers, Youth, Females, and Males.

The Great Mindset Divide

Before marketers approach any of the African-American segments, it is necessary to first understand The Great Divide, which puts most African Americans into either of two "umbrella" mindset segments. This separation falls along the pre- and post-Civil Rights era (1950s to late 1960s when the Civil Rights Movement peaked, and the early 1970s when some of the results from the Movement were more visible.). Most GenXers weren't born, or were too young to appreciate the struggle that Dr. King and the Civil Rights Movement endured in the Sixties. However, that time left an indelible mark on the hearts and in the minds of pre-Civil Rights era adults, born between 1940 and 1960.

Both pre- and post-Civil Rights consumers believe that "keepin' it real" is important to the preservation of Black culture because it identifies a range of natural sincerity about "staying close to your roots" that extends from being clear-cut and straightforward to brutally honest. If we were to view "keepin' it real" on a continuum, most Civil Rights-era Boomers' honesty mindset would land them toward the left of the spectrum—direct, yet safe and respectable. Many post-Civil Rights GenXers tend to land at the opposite end of the spectrum, shamelessly bold and realistic.

Keepin' It Real [35]

Boomers ⟵————————————⟶	GenXers
Seeking the truth and what's honest and living by those values. Telling the truth while being respectful of history, Black leaders, heroes, mothers, religion . . .	Sassiness, shamelessly bold and realistic. Being authentic and savvy. Being brutally honest—anything goes; nothing is sacred if it's the truth.

At this writing, a group of young African-American entrepreneurs (Akademiks) have used a racy campaign ("Read Books, Get Brain") for their popular clothing line. Their outdoor and transit ads targeted Black teens and tweens, and ran in Chicago, New York and other major African-American markets. Good idea? Not so fast. The entrepreneurs learned that among Black youth, the "Get Brain" expression is rapidly spreading underground because it is "coded language" or "city slang" for oral sex. Akademiks' strategy on the outside appears to justify promoting the importance of reading to Black youth. Perhaps these entrepreneurs are counting on the double meaning of the message to connect with the younger population in a way that communicates to them that Akademiks is hip, trendy, and knows how to "keep it real."

However, the Black community, led primarily by the Boomers and some GenXers, is retaliating. *The New York Times* reported that the Metropolitan Transit Authority ordered the ads removed from several trains and billboards in the New York area.[36] In Chicago, a letter-writing campaign to the Chicago Transit Authority (CTA) from nearly half of Trinity United Church of Christ's 12,000 members helped encourage the CTA to ban the campaign on its buses and trains. Additionally, shopping malls across the country, have banned the campaign and collectively these efforts have helped squash Akademiks' "Get Brain" efforts in several markets.[37]

Despite this nationwide backlash, Akademiks continues to boldly display the Get Brain campaign on its website. In support of Akademiks and the hip-hop culture, Howard University's *Hilltop* student newspaper printed the following point of view: "This ad is catchy and totally appropriate for the hip-hop clothing line. Hip-hop should be able to maintain a degree of flexibility and creativity without being criticized."[38]

A New Way to Be Black

Old School:

> We (African Americans) must learn how to be Black and function
> successfully in a white world . . . to act white to gain employment,
> without sacrificing the values of home and neighborhood. [41]
>
> —Lenora Fulani, political activist and educator

New School:

> *I don't want to wake up and be 45, overqualified and under-employed, and think how I got pimped.*
> —Sean Hudson, a 34-year-old African-American marketing executive at Bristol Meyers-Squibb

The late Ossie Davis, the thoughtful veteran actor seemed to take selected pages from both the Boomers' and GenXers' notebooks, when he announced to the African-American community, "What we need now is a new way to be Black!"[39]

Perceiving that the Boomer generation of African Americans adhered to the philosophy of having to work twice as hard, did everything necessary, and still did not become corporate leaders in large numbers, today's post-Civil Rights GenXers have embraced Davis' idea by living life on their own terms and not conforming to the patterns and behavior of the previous generation. Instead, they have learned how to be Black and function successfully in a white world. They have learned

The Great Mindset Divide

Baby Boomers *Born Before or During Civil Rights Era*	GenXers *Born After Civil Rights Era*
• High hopes for another "Dr. King"	• Dr. Martin Luther King, Jr. *who?*
• Maintaining culture most important	• Culture important, lifestyle also important
• Politically aware; largest group of political activists	• Involvement in political process becoming of growing importance via celebrities
• Moderate to high desire for instant gratification	• Highest propensity for instant gratification
• Race/racism very top-of-mind	• Largest segment of self-described bi-racials; higher propensity for inclusion
• Strongly against African-American stereotypes in the media	• Most likely to find some African-American stereotypes humorous, non-threatening
• All-Black cast very important, very top of mind	• All-Black cast important, but least top of mind

LESSONS LEARNED

Tapping into a New Way to Be Black

In an interview with *Salon.com*, Bakakari Kitwana, former political editor of *The Source* magazine, when explaining the political differences between older and younger African Americans, raised an interesting point about the mindset divide: "The older generation had not taken enough time to try to understand what is unique about the hip-hop generation."[40]

African Americans born after the Civil Rights Movement have an entirely different mindset of who they are as Black people in America. Understanding this distinction can have a dramatic impact on who, how, what, and, when you market to them.

Programs celebrating past Black achievements don't impact African-American GenXers as much as they do African-American Boomers.

African-American GenXers have new role models who don't strictly define themselves or restrict themselves by their Blackness. The people they admire are young, successful, savvy Black achievers who are making it on their own terms by using their Blackness in ways that give them more of a voice and control of their own destiny.

---

to achieve success without sacrificing the values of home and neighborhood. Many GenXers start with the belief that being successful doesn't mean emulating white success. Instead, they recognize that in this new global, more diverse society, their "Blackness" has value and can be a catalyst to achieving success, and building wealth.

The fact that the Fortune 500 has four Black CEOs is not necessarily a reason for these post-Civil Rights babies to celebrate. The few "appointed" Boomer African-American role models who have achieved success in corporate America are important, but are less impressive to many GenXers. They have new role models who are self-made and who, instead of having to mask their Blackness, have embraced it and leveraged it into wealth as entrepreneurs. Cora Daniels, author of *Black Power Inc.*, agrees and further explains the philosophy of the GenX

Marketing programs that resonate with this market segment will reflect an understanding and insider's affinity with the background and mind-set of this proud, savvy, and achievement-oriented segment.

Infiniti's "Infiniti in Black" internet marketing program is an example of a car company that understands how to effectively reach and talk to African-American GenXers who have discovered a new way to be Black. "Infiniti in Black" is a celebration of the African-American influencer. The very stylized side-by-side presentation uses a collection of double entendre meanings for words like "expression," "fusion," "vision," and "space" to describe both the entrepreneur and the car. This is executed with a split screen of video clips of artists and musicians displaying and talking about their craft on one side, and a Black Infiniti G-35 coupe on the other side. The site also invites viewers to return for upcoming presentations of future entrepreneurs and autos. The communication to African Americans is that Infiniti celebrates their accomplishments, supports their "living life on their own terms" mindset, and acknowledges that they are smart, cool, and hip. And here's the car to compliment that person and image.

mindset: "In their realistic view, race is something then, that cannot and will not be hidden. For the first time, a generation is willing to look away from the inequalities and mistreatment at large. By admitting that that they don't have the power to change things and make the field level, they are driven to succeed on their own."[41]

The transformation of self-made pop icons like P-Diddy, Jay Z, and Russell Simmons who have evolved from Black rap artists to world class entrepreneurs has given rise to the epiphany of *"a new way to be Black and achieve in America."* Russell Simmons emphatically states, "Our kids have a new entrepreneurial spirit. They're doing it. It's happening now. That's all they are talking about. Getting money. Owning companies. They are not talking about how brilliantly they rap: they are talking about how much money they are making and how they are making it. Legal money."[42] Further, Usher, America's 26-year-old "King of Pop" music proudly proclaimed his ownership share in an NBA team to 5,000 screaming fans at his concert in Puerto Rico by saying, "I am a musician, but I am a businessman first."[43]

The new reality for this generation of young African-American achievers is the opportunity to leverage their superior education, high visibility, insider access, and new found Blackness as "arbiters of cool" as stepping stones to a higher, longer-lasting level of achievement, success, and independence.

A Snapshot of African-American Youth: Indisputable Market Influencers

Today's youth, aged 8 to 20, are one of the most desperately sought after groups by marketers; and when marketers think of youth today, they see hip-hop as the youth market's natural appendage. The most visible impact on consumer taste is the addictive influence of the hip-hop culture and Black youth.

They are, more than any other segment, the developers of groundbreaking music and influencers of, and the authority for, innovative style. According to *Ebony* magazine, it was in imitation of Black hip-hop culture that the chief character on *Sex in the City* thought it was cool to wear gold name plates around her neck. African-American youth were fashionably chic in velour jogging suits back in the 1980s, long before Juicy Couture, and they taught dictionary makers how to spell "bootylicious."[44]

Hip-hop culture originated in the mid 1970s among African-American and Latino youth in New York City. Hip-hop was a means to express their "lived experiences" often of life in the ghetto. For African Americans, the music was a way to authenticate their Black identity to other Black youth. Some of these youth became activists; others became musicians and rap artists who wore street gear of heavy gold chains. And later, when they became successful, and because of The Filter, they upgraded to designer labels such as Tommy Hilfiger, Donna Karan, and Gucci—symbols of their success.[45] Today, hip-hop has exploded and crossed racial lines. It represents over 100 million consumers and $300 billion in buying power[46] and has become a ubiquitous phenomenon driven by music, style, language and culture, primarily fueled by Black youth.

Black Teens

*It is possible that cornrows and braids will gain the same popularity
in the mainstream that the ponytail once enjoyed.*[47]
—*Africana.com*, January 2004

African-American teens are very important to marketers because they
serve as the cool, hip models for their peers. Black teens' desire to stand
out from the crowd rather than blend into it is a value that most likely
inspired fashions (baggy jeans, baseball caps on backwards, and oversized shirts), hairstyles (cornrows/braids), musical taste (rap/hip-hop)
and other preferences that have been adopted by teens of other races.
In addition to the point made earlier, Lafayette Jones, CEO of
Segmented Marketing Services Inc (SMSi), a retail merchandising, marketing and publishing company, associates this effect with widespread
influence. "While most teens influence family purchases, African-American teens influence a whole culture."[48]

Film critic Roger Ebert noted in his review of *The Matrix Reloaded*
that the use of so many African–American actors is in sharp contrast
with past science-fiction films that plopped one or two African-American
characters in the story, such as Billy Dee Williams in the *Return of the
Jedi*. "The [directors] . . . use so many African Americans . . . because
to the white teenagers who are the primary audience for this movie,

Black Youth's Influence and Spending Power[49]

- African-American teens influence $164 billion annually that fuels the total youth market.

- Seven million Black youths between 8 and 18 years old spend 6 percent per month more in general than the average American counterpart—about $428 monthly per person.

> Black teens spend more on clothes and fine jewelry.

- Black youth spend more annually on items such as clothing, jewelry, computer software, and athletic footwear when compared with all U.S. teens. In fact, Black teens spend $329 on average per person per year on apparel, or 18 percent more than the $280 annual average per person by all U.S. teens.

- On average Black teens spend $233 a year on fine jewelry or 40 percent more than the $166 per person average for all teens.

African Americans embody a cool, a cachet, an authenticity . . . "[50]

Ebony magazine supports Jones' and Ebert's observations in one of its articles on Black youth when they reported that "Black American youth created rap, hip-hop and almost every other major pop development of the last 20 years. They exert a major influence over the music radio stations play, the movies that get produced, the commercials that air, the fashions on the runways, the songs we sing, and the dance moves that white icons like Britney Spears make."[51]

Erik Parker, music editor of *Vibe* magazine, which chronicles hip-hop life, notes that Def Jam, the largest hip-hop record label, has offices in Germany and France to take advantage of the expanding hip-hop culture. "A lot of European countries have white kids who adapt hip-hop to their own culture," says Parker.[52]

Tweens

Tweens, 8 to 14 years old, are one of the most sought after groups by marketers, according to Packaged Facts' research study, *The U.S. Tween Market*. In general, *most* tweens:

- Are growing up more quickly, both physically and emotionally, than children in generations past.[53]
- Are more brand-conscious and fashion conscious than teens.
- Have been deeply affected by one of the most significant changes in society, the decline in the proportion of traditional married-couple families and the increase in the number of families with a non-traditional structure.
- Still support traditional values, emphasizing the importance of family, religion, and community service.
- Are more comfortable using information technology and personal electronics products;
- Exhibit an interest in electronic media and engage in multitasking as a matter of routine.[54]

Although older teens, aged 15 to 19 are more likely to search for self-identity and independence, most tweens feel very close to their parents, especially to their mothers—whether biological or not.[55] Tweens often inform their households about the "latest and greatest" technologies and trends, then use "pester power" to influence product and

Black Teen Support Can Mean the Difference Between Success or Failure for a Fashion Line

The following excerpt from a 2002 *Colorlines* article provides an example of Black teen influence in the fashion industry.

Over ten years ago, when Gap Inc. and Levi Strauss & Co. gazed into the future of their clothing empires, youth of color were an irrelevant demographic. For years, those images, alternately flashy and sexy and subdued, were above all, white. . . . In its marketing, Gap focused on selling khakis to the predominately white professional class and their children and Levi's left the power of its name on autopilot, selling denim to teenagers in department stores.

"From Sweatshop to Hip-Hop: Once Ignored by Fashion, Youth of Color Become the Focus of Its Marketing," by Ryan Pitado-Vertner, *Colorlines* Magazine, Summer 2002

Like most of the fashion industry Gap and Levi's were more than a decade late on hip-hop. They gambled against hip-hop and lost millions. . . . Both companies suffered from a loss of cool. . . . Then, after hip-hop exploded in the 1990s, reality slapped them right in the face. They finally got the hint and the shift was evident on television commercials and billboards across the county. Since 1997, Gap has featured L.L. Cool, J. Missy Elliot, India Arie, and Macy Gray. Levi focused its attention on progressive artists by promoting a Lauryn Hill concert tour. They also promoted Mos Def and the Black Eyed Peas.

Tommy Hilfiger listened . . . and was among the first mainstream fashion icons to cash in on the hip-hop strategy. Hilfiger's traditional marketing strategy relied on heavy doses of American patriotism, sharp-jawed white men and New England atmosphere. But one day African-American hip-hop influencers discovered the brand and Tommy was suddenly, almost effortlessly, the epitome of cool.

Making that impressionable stamp on the teen market today can have tremendous rewards for marketers in the future.

service purchases, including vehicles, cellular telephones, electronics, groceries, and vacations.

Little is published about Black tweens. However they, like their older African-American siblings, have tremendous influence among their tween peers.

Marketers should pay close attention to Black tweens. Not only are they among the tweens estimated to have $39 billion in personal spending power, but they can also influence the $300 billion that is spent in response to pester power.[62] Given their trendsetter characteristic, they are prime targets for new and innovative products and services.

Black tweens are aware of advertisers' efforts, and are more likely to be responsive if the messages are culturally relevant, and appeal to their aspirations. This is especially true if the messages address their need to differentiate themselves from others. For example, Black tweens like culturally relevant television shows. Nickelodeon's *Romeo!* with rappers Romeo and his father Master P. *Romeo!* was the number one cable show among Black tweens during 2003–2004, while *SpongeBob SquarePants* was popular with the general market.[56]

In fact, African-American tweens who "live Black," i.e., reside, socialize, and worship in Black communities, are more likely to maintain Black cultural habits than those African-American tweens who live in mixed or predominately white communities. The importance of keeping the Black cultural connection alive for Black children in predomi-

The Differences Between Black and White Tweens

The desire to stand out from the crowd rather than blend into it is a value more frequently expressed by African-American youth than Anglo youth, according to Burrell Communications' *Burrell Barometer*. Additionally, Black tweens:

- Grew in numbers at more than twice the rate of white tweens (16 percent versus 7.4 percent) from 1997 to 2002, according to the U.S. Census Bureau.[57]

- Are more likely to be urban dwellers, as 51.6 percent lived in central cities in 2002 compared with 23.1 percent of white tweens and are more likely to reside in single-parent households (52 percent) compared with white tweens (23 percent) and the households are usually headed by their mothers (47.4 percent).[58]

> **Black tweens have more influence on family vacations.**

- Have more influence on family vacations (30 percent vs. 22 percent of the general market).[59]

- At the same time, Black tweens are more likely to be punished for bad grades (33.3 percent versus 5.6 percent of whites) and conversely, are more likely to be satisfied with their home life compared with white tweens (50 percent versus 34 percent).[60]

- Watch more TV compared with white tweens: (6 hours or more per day) or Hispanic peers (4 or more hours per day).[61]

nately white and prosperous suburbs of California is discussed in a qualitative study conducted by Beverly Daniel Tatum. According to Tatum, on the issue of developing racial identity, "I found that most parents were concerned about the impact of living in a white community, and in particular of attending predominantly white schools. Within this context, some parents adopted a race-conscious family frame, actively seeking out Black playmates for their children and encouraging involvement in Black cultural activities whenever possible in order to promote a more positive Black identity in their children."[62]

The Power of the African-American Female

African-American women represent a dominant consumer buying group in America. Their spending power and desire for high quality products and services makes them a coveted segment of buyers for virtually any organization seeking to grow market share.
—Miriam Muléy, CEO, *The 85% Niche: Rallying the Power of Women for Exponential Business Growth*

An article in *Women's Wear Daily* begins by discussing the buying power of African-American females, stating that they spent over $4 billion on apparel alone in 2000, and $7.6 billion when accessories were included. This was a 31 percent increase over 1999.[63] The article then goes on to proudly announce that it's "no longer about race for African Americans" and cites several industry expert opinions stating that targeting African-American women specifically is "absurd."[64]

The author of the *WWD* article not only missed the point about African-American female spending power but also, and perhaps more importantly, overlooked the fact that African-American women represent a powerful consumer group. In addition to representing a strong and upwardly mobile group of 19.1 million with spending power in excess of $403 billion in 2005, African-American women are the means for reaching the entire Black market.[65]

According to a new study by market research publisher Packaged Facts, *The U.S. African-American Market*, the aggregate income of Black women is equal to 49 percent of the total income of the Black population while Latino and non-Latino white women account for only around one-third of aggregate income for their respective groups.[66]

African-American women are young, educated, motivated, and visible in all aspects of society. Black females are more likely to be the primary decision-makers in their households. They are concerned about financial security, so they plan for the future. African-American women are also taking the entrepreneurial leap. African-American women-owned businesses are growing at a rate of four times the national average. As of 2004, there were an estimated 414,472 privately held firms with majority interest owned by African-American women in the U.S., employing more than 250,000 people and generating nearly $20 billion in sales according to the National Women's Business Council.[67]

Because they want to look and feel good, African-American women spend a higher percentage of their income on beauty and hair care products and services to fulfill these needs, compared with other women. This group will pay more for luxury brand names that serve as quality control and reflect their aspirations. As a result of their independence, confidence, mindset, and style, African-American women have tremendous influencing power in the marketplace. For example, *Vogue* magazine, which is targeted to primarily white females, may be the style standard for older women, but many younger females want to create their own styles. Therefore, both Black and white females often look to hip-hop or "urban" influenced styles as a way to be distinguished. Thus, when a multicultural young women's magazine with a heavy Black influence, like the recently departed *Suede*, puts a successful Black female celebrity like Eve, on the cover, the ability to reach segments beyond Black consumers is phenomenal. Carol H. Williams, CEO of Carol H. Williams Advertising, specializes in the African-American market and refers to this dynamic from the African-American market as "selling to and selling through."

The new marketing focus—to seek commonality among cultures—is particularly relevant among marketers who target women. The women's segment has received a particular boost by women marketing trendsetters and gurus of the 20th and 21st centuries. Faith Popcorn's *EVEolution* and *The Popcorn Report*, Mary Lou Quinlan's, *Just Ask a Woman*, and Martha Barletta's *Marketing to Women* have helped widen the direction with new insights, possibilities and a stronger rationale for targeting women. While many women do indeed have more in common than not, conspicuously absent from these discussions are key cultural differences that distinguish African-American women from their white female counterparts, the primary base group for many of the observations made by Ms. Popcorn, Quinlan, and Barletta.

These cultural characteristics make all the difference in determining whether marketing programs and communications are relevant to African-American women.

Black Women Reject General Market Beauty Standards

Given that women in general, are the drivers for the beauty and fashion industries, it is interesting that in spite of disproportionate amounts spent on clothing, hair care, and cosmetics by African-American women, their choices of colors, fabrics, and styles may contradict traditional beauty and current fashion ideals. African-American women's reluctance to give in to predominant culture fashion trends while also embracing their own style and bodies, has motivated the fashion industry to take heed, learn, and incorporate some of these styles in their product lines.

For as long as we can remember—years before "bootylicious"—Black women have celebrated their curvy figures. Research studies have shown that Black women "pay little attention to images of thin, white women."[68] In a recent article, Mikki Taylor, beauty director at *Essence* magazine states that when Black consumers watch television there is "not a yearning on the part of the audience to look like any other culture" citing the wide range of ideals of beauty among Black culture. "There just isn't a Black standard of beauty to live up to. We celebrate our uniqueness."[69]

Two separate research studies measured effectiveness of advertising on Black women. One study, conducted by the University of Michigan, looked at the influence of popular television on Black women. Another, by the University of Missouri, studied the effects that magazine ads featuring attractive images of white and Black young women played in shaping the self-image of Black women. Both studies concluded that Black women have better body images than white women, despite being heavier, though perhaps less healthy, than their white counterparts.[70] A University of South Carolina study found that African-American women indicated less desire to be a smaller size than did Caucasian women.

There are a variety of reasons why African-American women are generally heavier than white women. These reasons include, but are not limited to, socioeconomic factors, cultural expectations and norms, diet, and lack of regular exercise. Also:

- Weight isn't a big issue in the Black community. African Americans are less apt to belittle a full-figured woman.

- African-American women don't view the excess pounds as negatively as white women.

- African-American teenage girls are less likely to suffer from eating disorders such as anorexia and bulimia.[71]

In addition to the reasons listed above and stories about African heritage and genetics, the greater acceptance of their bodies is most likely attributed to the admiration by many Black men. The following quote from African-American author, April Sinclair, who writes novels about African-American characters and their experiences, provides an example of how many Black women associate the importance of their body image with the approval by Black men.

Girlfriend, you need to come on back home to the soulful south side
. . . it's plenty of men on the south side who like full-figured women.
—Sarita to Daphne Dupree[72]

Further, shapely African-American women are primarily featured in publications like *Black Men, Smooth,* and *King,* which have a large, though not exclusively African-American, male readership. According to *DiversityInc.com*, these magazines cater to "those who aren't drawn in by the likes of Paris Hilton." These so-called "thick" women present an alternative to the stereotypical waif-like cover models and are redefining beauty for a browning America.[73] Ralph Pucci, president of a mannequin design company, believes that the waif-like body image is losing popularity in the fashion industry and society in general. "If you look at the magazines, the girls are a little bit fuller. I don't think everyone has to be thin to be sexy anymore."[74]

Furthermore, mannequins with fuller breasts and hips are beginning to show up on the sales floors of Macy's and Filenes.[75] Urban clothing designer Mark Ecko was seeking a pant form with a more ample bottom to display his jeans. Since the installation of the new fuller-figured mannequins, sales of the EckoRed collection have tripled, according to Reuters. Creative director for Life Style Form and Display Company, Rich Rollinson believes that the popularity of more curvaceous celebrities like Jennifer Lopez and R&B singer Beyonce is empowering women to feel good about all different body types. He is

Coca-Cola Celebrates African-American Beauty

The Coca-Cola Company has targeted marketing and communications to the African-American community for over 30 years. During the 1990s, Burrell Communications created a very successful television campaign for Coke that demonstrated real inclusion and respect for African Americans.

One particular commercial depicted an African-American model that was in appearance, with her dark skin and close-cropped natural hair, the antithesis of what many African Americans perceive as white America's standard of beauty—white skin, blue eyes and blonde hair. The script called for her to say, "The ad said they were looking for the all American girl. So, what do you think?"

> Uniquely Black beauty is recognized, equal, respected, and appreciated.

This commercial, along with similar ones from the campaign were immensely successful with the African-American community. The model's appearance along with copy line was a profound statement to the African-American community, and particularly women, that Black beauty was recognized, equal, respected, and appreciated by a huge white-owned company that is considered an icon of America.

currently working with several urban clothing lines that appreciate a fuller mannequin.

Queen Latifah (aka Dana Owens), as celebrity spokesperson for Cover Girl Cosmetics, has sent an obvious invitation to African-American women and other women of size. However, according to research studies with African-American women, prior to Latifah, many Black women believed the long standing "easy, breezy beautiful Cover Girl" tagline was confirmation of the beauty that Cover Girl's white, blue-eyed models conveyed for years. However, today, Latifah and Cover Girl talk to a diverse audience that embraces Black beauty and women who celebrate being sexy, happy, and full-figured.

The Opportunity

When I see sisters who look like me, or people I know, I tune in and focus on your product and say to myself, "They actually went to the trouble to look for me."

—Jill Nelson, author, *Finding Martha's Vineyard*

Cultivating the African-American female consumer could determine the success of your brand. However, African-American women continue to be undervalued by many marketers who opt to promote their products and services via universal behavioral characteristics. In addition to providing *entrée* into the broader $761 billion African-American consumer market as mentioned earlier, marketing executives fail to grasp that African-American women are more likely to control the purse strings in their households than white women as reflected in the data in the sidebar "The Primary Decision-maker." Thus, besides setting fashion trends that are created from placing a high priority on defining their personal style, these women are prime targets for financial and investment products and services, automobiles, electronics, travel, personal care products and services, as well as clothing, and accessories.

Additionally, when the Missouri School of Journalism studied the effect that ads featuring attractive images of young white and Black women had on shaping the self-image of Black women, the participants dismissed images of attractive white women as unimportant, but they were affected by images of attractive Black women.[76] This suggests that a strategy that identifies differences and relevant "talking to me" characteristics is more likely to compel these valuable African-American consumers to take action.

These are just a few of the many examples that demonstrate that while African-American women are participating in lifestyle activities that are similar to mainstream America, they are most strongly influenced by messages that speak to them as Black women—by models, spokespersons, and actresses who look like them. The uniqueness and variety of these relevant marketing and communication ideals are most often viewed within an African-American paradigm, rather than among the diversities of the general population.

The Good News About African-American Men

Black men are the ultimate in masculinity; adored and desired, but feared at the same time.
            —Courtney Kemp-Agboh, staff writer, *The Bernie Mac Show*

African Americans perceive that Black men, in particular, are highly scrutinized by white media and the general public, and tend to be

The Primary Decision-maker [77]

Across many key categories, African-American women are more likely than white women to be the primary decision-maker in their households, according to a 2005 study by Liberman Research and The Hunter-Miller Group for *Essence* magazine.

	African-American Females	White Females
Travel	50%	42%
Financial Services/Investments	41	33
Real Estate	32	24
Home electronics	45	38
Automobiles	36	30

Additionally, African-American women:

- In married households, are more likely to be the primary decision-makers when buying a house; one in two married Black women versus one in four married white women.[78]

> African-American women are the primary decision-makers in their households and businesses

- Are professionally advancing, assuming powerful positions in business, law, medicine, and other fields.

- Are more likely than women of other races to be business owners.

- Regularly change some aspect of their style (clothing or hair); 28 percent compared with 8 percent of white women.

- Most likely spent the majority of $20 billion dollars on beauty products consumed by all African-Americans in 2003.[79]

- Seek investments individually, or through clubs and other means, to save for the future.

- Read an average of 16.5 magazines each month, compared with 12.2 magazines read by women overall.[80]

- Importantly, of women who rely on magazines as a source of information, 70 percent rely on African-American magazines, while only 5 percent rely on general market magazines.

negatively stereotyped. What is not published or promoted enough is the good news about Black men.

African-American men have made significant advances despite the perpetuation of negative stereotypes. This group has been growing at three times the rate of the white male population; they are younger with a median age of 28.5 compared with 35.3 years for the general population. And because African-American males are younger, their life expectancy has been on the rise.

Their college enrollment increased 38.8 percent between 1990 and 2000, as education becomes a means for overcoming some societal barriers and advancing oneself. Additionally African-American men are taking more responsibility for their families; two-parent families increased at nearly double the U.S. rate from 1990 to 2000.

And many have assumed significant roles in business, politics, sports, entertainment and other arenas. In turn, education and professional achievements have had an impact on their incomes with a 59.7 percent gain in mean earnings between 1990 and 2000.[81] Additionally, from a psychographic standpoint, African-American men are:

- Less likely to feel that mainstream marketing speaks to their lifestyles. Many African-American males tend to be more political and cynical and therefore tend to criticize those communications that do not speak specifically to them.[82]

- Concerned with personal advancement as exemplified by their pursuit of higher education and significant memberships in professional and trade organizations, both African-American and mainstream.

- Technologically savvy, using the internet for a wide variety of tasks and being among the first to try new electronic products.

- The ultimate originators of "cool," an important marketing characteristic often copied by whites and other cultures.

Highlighting the Good News About African-American Men

In order to reach the head, you must first touch the heart.
—Samuel J. Chisholm, President, Chisholm Consulting, Inc.

The importance of this younger and growing male population must not be overshadowed by negative stereotypes. African-American men are a

The Influential Cool Factor

They are intimidated by us, but they imitate us.
    —Ron Miller, African-American Real Estate Broker

Despite their often-bad rap, Black men continue to be the influential drivers of many of the trends associated with pop culture. The cool cachet is one of the most marketable characteristics primarily inspired by Black men.

Marlene Kim Connor provides an interesting look at "cool" and its role towards the development of the Black man's persona, in her book *What Is Cool? Understanding Black Manhood in America.* She writes:

> "The word cool has been adopted in the mainstream as a term that describes anybody who marches to the beat of a different drummer, who blazes trails, who follows no trends, who is sexy, alone, mysterious, hip self-assured, different, quiet, confident, rebellious. . . . Cool is perhaps the most important force in the life of a Black man in America. . . . Cool is not just a term, it is a lifestyle. It has little to do with the hippest clothes or the latest fad. Cool became the new rules and new culture for those Black people who rejected white American culture and white America's notions of how people behave. The language is different, the symbols are different, and finally the men themselves are different."

> **Cool is perhaps the most important force in the life of a Black man in America**

She describes this attitude that evolved from the "street cool" in Black communities as, "a down-to-earth attitude of self-confidence; knowing that you can handle yourself."[84]

Symbols of cool may begin with clothes, but it definitely ends with attitude.

critical market segment with substantial buying power that continues to increase at a notable rate. One approach for marketers who want to tap into this market is to recognize the "Black man's burden" by avoiding the perpetuation of stereotypes.

From qualitative research, we have learned that marketers will elicit positive response from most African Americans when they depict positive images of Black men with families and in leadership roles, i.e., showing them as a respected family head and concerned father, business owner, corporate executive—an all-around good guy.

An example of translating the "Black man's burden" aspect of the Black experience to an effective marketing strategy is Burrell Communications' targeted campaign for Proctor and Gamble's Tide brand. The campaign features an African-American man sleeping on his back with a small child sleeping on his stomach. There's a shiny gold wedding band on his left hand and neo-soul music playing softly in the background. Burrell and P&G took on an important issue in the Black community—the perception that all Black men are absent fathers—and made it positive and relevant.

According to Sarah Patterson, VP Director of Research and Account Planning for Burrell Communications, the campaign is receiving "rave reviews" from the Black community because it truly uplifts and gives Black men (and the Black community) their due by demonstrating the "normalcy" that occurs within the Black lifestyle." Moreover, because the African-American community received the campaign so positively, Burrell and P&G decided to also include the ads in their general market rotation. As a result, according to P&G's Tide brand team, the commercial has the highest performance score among other Tide commercials, and the brand achieved the highest return on investment as a result of that commercial.

Make no mistake, if the Burrell campaign had featured an all-white cast, the response would have been dramatically different for African Americans. It most likely would have been just another white spot and would have done little or nothing for the Black community. This spot demonstrated an insider's knowledge of the African-American mindset by dispelling a major stereotype about Black men. In addition to the high scores and ROI that the campaign achieved, it will likely enhance the loyalty African Americans have for the brand by creating greater awareness through retention and word-of-mouth.

SIX

"Yes, We Speak English, but You <u>Still</u> Aren't Talking to Us."

*You can say the right thing about a product and nobody will listen.
You've got to say it in a way that people will feel in their gut. Because
if they don't feel it, nothing will happen.*
—William Bernbach, co-founder, Doyle Dane Bernbach

Although a marketer's message may be understood, it may not be relevant to African-American individuals and thus, will not stimulate the desired response. This lack of response from African-American consumers is what makes millions of marketing dollars ineffective. Determining the most effective way to reach the Black consumer is largely based on the following:

- Acknowledging their cultural filters
- Using language and lifestyle situations that are relevant to them and their culture
- Understanding their value as influencers
- Choosing marketing and media strategies that are relevant in the community

In order to understand African-American interpretations and reactions to marketing messages, you should note some sensitivities regarding African-American communications.

Raising the B.A.R.

After more than 20 years of helping advertisers develop effective advertising to African Americans, we have identified three basic requirements for doing it successfully, i.e., motivating the consumer to try or buy:

Believability — Is it true, does it make sense? Is it too much of a stretch or leap of faith?

Appealing — Is it eye catching, does it have stopping power? Is it attractive and visually gratifying?

Relevant — What's Black about it? Does the advertising depict something African Americans can relate to or identify with, minus stereotypical images?

Additionally,

When marketing to African Americans, most value self-image, style, and intellect. However, many are also at the same time very literal when it comes to communications. In advertising, it is what it is, and it needs to make sense straight away, or it will be passed over. Given many African Americans' propensity for instant gratification, requiring this target to figure out a message may result in not receiving any message at all.

About me, but not by me

As mentioned earlier, some African Americans cite and criticize other African Americans for stereotyping the African-American community. However, over the years we have observed that most African Americans are likely to believe that African-American images portrayed in the common media—media that is familiar and used daily—are controlled primarily by decision-makers who are mostly non-African Americans. Essentially, these portrayals are second hand. Here are some comments from our focus groups:

- "Our portrayal is controlled by those with the power."
- "The decision makers who 'green light' the stories the public sees are not African Americans. So there is a lack of sensitivity to what is offensive to our culture."
- "What we mostly see in the media about Blacks seems to be filtered through someone else's eyes and experiences about what they think Black people are supposed to be about, as opposed to feeling that it is being created by an actual Black person."
- "It's like we are materialistic with no sense of values . . . we are painted with a brush that shows we have no understanding of what's really valuable in the world."
- "We are portrayed as a culture with no real depth . . . it's just about the materialist things . . . singing, dancing, being funny, and

doing sports . . . but our intelligence and our families are just dealt with on a superficial level."[85]

While moderating Rainbow/PUSH Wall Street's Project panel, "Media Power—Shaping and Misshaping the Image of Minorities," Luke Visconti, partner and co-founder of DiversityInc.com made this observation:

"The image of people of color influences how the people of power perceive people of color. If a banker or broker has a perception that people of color represent a marginal market, then there's going to be no rush to open the door. On the other hand, if a broker or banker perceive that a quarter of the market in this country has household income that is growing at more than twice the rate of that of the other three-quarters of the market, then there will be a rush to open the door."[86]

"Why Can't They Just Show Us Normal?"

The comment above was made in an African-American focus group and encapsulates how many African Americans desire to see themselves in the collective media. Given African-Americans' increased visibility in the media, many perceive that African Americans are targets for negative and erroneous stereotypes.

"The lens though which people learn about races is absolutely though TV, not through human contact," says Charles Gallagher, sociologist at Georgia State University in Atlanta. "Ads make it seem that race doesn't matter, when real life would tell you something different."[87]

Some African Americans believe that within the last 5 to 10 years, there has been some improvement in how Blacks are portrayed in the media, but they also believe that these portrayals are not quite there, and therefore, the media situation is still negative overall:

- "Things are only marginally better now than they were five or ten years ago because we are starting to see African Americans in roles and contexts that affect everyone, not just Blacks. Ten years ago, the only time you saw Blacks on the news in a positive way was because they were talking about civil rights."

- "We are doing better but we are not portrayed by the media as doing better."

- "What we see about Blacks is an illusion because 10 years ago you just heard about the bottom 5 percent of us, but now it's the bottom 5 percent and the top 5 percent, which includes the athletes and the rappers, but it's still not a realistic picture of us."

- "Things are a little better now than they were five years ago, but they're still negative overall."

Not to refute the point we made earlier, marketers' desire to depict multi-racial images in advertising may be fueled by the comments of some African Americans. In focus group sessions, when asked what types of people they like to see in advertising, some African Americans will describe a politically correct racial balance of Blacks, whites and other ethnic groups. White respondents were less likely to describe that balance.

We have observed that the impact of The Filter may cause many African Americans to feel they are excluded from particular opportunities, and their desire for inclusion is heightened. When those same Black respondents were asked which advertising messages grab their attention, nearly all agreed that ads depicting an all-Black cast spoke best to them. They further qualified their answers by saying that situations that speak directly to them should be non-stereotypical, positively reflect who they are, and connect them to the African-American culture. This will get, and keep, their attention every time.

Advertising Black History Month

I was thinking the store was celebrating Black History Month. Then I looked further down the flier [sic] and saw that they were advertising Tone bar soap … and cornbread mix … I thought, "No, they didn't!" [95]

—Middle school teacher's reaction to the Kmart flyer, "Celebrate Black History"

Many advertisers have jumped on the Black History Month bandwagon, creating a new selling cycle during the short, slow retail month of February. Magazine ads, special circulars and broadcast messages salute Black History Month, offer factoids about "famous, important, or heroic" African Americans and their achievements in history, while offering products and services geared toward the African-American con-

Advertising Black History Month 101

What helps people, helps business.
—Leo Burnett, founder, Leo Burnett Worldwide

McDonald's launched a multi-tiered Black History campaign on February 1, 2002. Created to encourage continued celebration of African American History in the month of February and beyond, the overall creative platform for the campaign centered on the question, "What month do you celebrate Black History?"

The national initiative, branded "365 Black," includes displaying a commemorative, poster in all U.S. restaurants, new radio and television commercial spots featuring nationally syndicated radio personality, Tom Joyner, and print ads appearing in _American Legacy, Ebony, Jet, Savoy_ and _Upscale_ magazines throughout the year.

In addition to having Joyner appear in commercials, McDonald's is the 52-week sponsor of the segment called "Little Known Black History Facts" (LKBHF). LKBHF is a daily feature on the _Tom Joyner Morning Show_, a nationally syndicated urban radio program heard in more than 100 markets. Each morning, Joyner highlights a little-known fact about African Americans.

> A celebration of Black history can occur in any month.

The _Tom Joyner Morning Show_ is the most popular radio program among U.S. African Americans. There is no mention of Big Macs®, fries, or Egg McMuffins® throughout the entire campaign. They don't need to be mentioned. African Americans know what McDonald's sells. The fact that McDonald's has made a continuing commitment to honoring Black History, and toward the African-American market in general, along with spending dollars on Black radio, is very powerful.

Obviously, not every company has McDonald's money. But money is not why this campaign works. What works is that it is an unselfish campaign, offering benefits to the audience without directly asking anything in return.[88]

sumer. While many African-American consumers appreciate marketers' recognition of their history and culture, many have also challenged marketers to embrace Black history more often than once a year.

Some marketing experts are not surprised by this trend in attitudes by African-American consumers. According to Barbara Lippert, ad critic for *Adweek* magazine, "Eventually any piece of history or American culture gets trivialized by advertisers." She added, "Advertisers have a long history of 'exploiting' history to sell products."[89]

While some companies do develop ads that pay tribute to Black History Month without mentioning products, others need to be sensitive about trying to exploit African-American history to promote and sell their products. A well-intentioned, but product-intensive message may be perceived as disrespectful or insulting by the very segment that the message was intended to reach.

Civil rights activists and educators are becoming increasingly uncomfortable with the commercial exploitation of the holiday, originally intended to honor the history of Black achievement in America. Like the teacher quoted above, African-American consumers are becoming more aware of the ulterior motives of some of these promotions.

Advertisers who genuinely want to celebrate Black History Month, and who produce thoughtful, informative messages may gain more brand equity by not emphasizing their products. The PBS series on slavery by Ken Burns, sponsored by General Motors, is a good example.

African Americans See More, and See Differently

In 1990, Dr. Robert Pitts, marketing professor at Chicago's De Paul University, conducted a survey among African-American and white consumers to help resolve two misconceptions that marketing executives had about African-American consumers.

- Blacks and whites can be reached in the same way.
- An all-Black cast offends white audiences.

After showing to African-American and white consumers the same four television commercials featuring an all-Black cast, the research revealed: African Americans see more and whites see less. Some scenarios from the commercials depicted dual-parent family situations, a nicely dressed couple or single person buying a new car. Thus, according to the study:

"What whites fail to see is very evident to the Black audience. Whites fail to realize certain social, respect and accomplishment values present

Some Insider Help with the Opportunity

In this digital age, the phrase, "having a Kodak moment" is a bit dated, but it still reminds us how advertising often portrays more sentimentality and good heartedness than what actually occurs in life. In part, the strategic intent of such advertising is rooted in the theory that seeing ourselves in a good light can translate into goodwill towards the advertiser. While this has universally human merit, it is more poignantly the case with Blacks. Perceptions and residual effects from The Filter have influenced many African Americans to see themselves and other Blacks as having lesser value than, particularly, whites (again, the equality issue). Very few will admit this publicly, but their actions and mindset say otherwise. There is an unpopular but well-known saying in the Black community that supports this observation about personal value: "Black folks believe the white man's ice is colder." Although volumes could be written on the value issues connected to that quote, our point here is a simple one: African Americans need more Kodak moments.

> There is a need to build trust within the African-American community.

To that end, portraying Black-on-Black altruism would serve well. We have observed, in both personal experience and research, that African Americans often comment about not sufficiently helping or trusting one another and not treating each other fairly. It's one of the "dirty laundry" issues unknown or not recognized by marketers and is not discussed publicly outside the African-American community.

A late 1990's study for General Motors and a 2002 study for Focus on the Family, the Christian organization, both asked African-American respondents about issues that plague the African-American community. Besides the typical responses that included the lack of good education, crime, drugs, and teen/parent scenarios, nearly all cited the issue concerning the need to increase trust with each other. Therefore, when clients ask us for recommendations on how to avoid the pitfalls of negative stereotyping in portrayals of African Americans, we suggest they consider scenarios in which people are helping one another, giving emotional support, offering sage advice, and being appreciated for their efforts.

in some advertising. An important aspect of the Black experience is the struggle for fulfillment, belonging, accomplishment and respect in a white-dominated culture."[90]

The study also suggests that whites are not offended by all-Black representations. Whites reacted almost as positively toward the tested advertising as Blacks; only the takeaway was different.

Fifteen years later, the De Paul study findings continue to reign as a powerful marketing reality that struggles against the beliefs and mind-set of marketers who fail to see the positive values that African Americans often look for and see in advertising, and whites who are not turned off by these depictions. In similar studies with Black and white audiences who have viewed the same commercials, the results continue to be the same as in the DePaul study more than 15 years earlier.

The above illustrates the effect of *The Filter*—what is simply accepted by whites is very significant and valuable to Blacks.

SEVEN

"Media for the People"[91]

There is an efficient way to reach African-American consumers—through Black media. Like the general market, African Americans use various types of media, but unlike the general market, they embrace Black media. African-American media serve seven key functions for the Black community:

- Provide news
- Serve as leaders and influencers
- Provide credibility
- Be trustworthy sources
- Educate
- Give voice to African Americans
- Speak to African Americans in a culturally appropriate manner

What makes these seven characteristics unique for the Black community is that Black media provide the added value of the person-to-person emotional factor not typically delivered to the Black community by general market media. Black media have more credibility than general market media and deliver and add authority and weight to the "influencer contacts" within the Black community.

"When a person makes the cover of *N'Digo* (a respected, established Black "magapaper" in Chicago), the whole community takes notice!" says a devoted reader. *N'Digo* Publisher Hermene Hartman, who also publishes the national publication *N'Digo Profiles*, and has recently relaunched *Savoy* magazine, adds: "The *N'Digo* cover, in its *Vogue* likeness is power! Power because it clearly states someone has taken the time and sensitivity to make an impact and not be casual. This is important because we don't see ourselves like that enough in the general market media. We are starved for positive media images. Too often, the general market media portrays us at our worst. What we often see is the negative criminal in the general market media."

Studies have proven that African-Americans are more receptive to targeted messages in Black media. In one study among African-American respondents, led by Bendixen & Associates, 79 percent indicated that they rely on news and information from Black media sources.[92] Further, 56 percent of respondents agreed with the statement: "I pay more attention to commercials that run during TV programs with an all-Black cast."[93]

Given that more African Americans are using general market media today, it's no wonder that the primary strategy for many marketers is to focus more on lifestyle, and reach these consumers via general marketing media and communications. However, many companies underestimate the impact and value of African-American media with less than 1 percent (approximately 0.68 percent) of annual advertising expenditures ($1.8 billion) being devoted to these media that focus on a $761 billion market.[94]

"Minority-owned media outlets are critical for minorities to have their voices heard in an undiluted manner" according to the National Association of Black Owner Broadcasters.[95] Darius Evans, a partner at GTM, a multicultural communications firm, further emphasizes the importance of Black media outlets to the Black community, "Black folks are still going to identify with Black folks. That's why *BET, Essence, Ebony, Savoy, Black Enterprise,* and other Black outlets are important. We constantly need to enhance our sense of self."[96]

The sections that follow provide an overview and some stats of the various types of media that have been successful when targeting African-American consumers.

Radio

African Americans listen to a lot of radio—22.3 hours per week. Moreover, radio reaches 95.1 percent of African Americans aged 12 and older each week, making it the top medium for this market segment.[97] Brad Sanders, President of Babysitters Production, and veteran producer and voice of TV One and syndicated radio shows "On the Phone with Ti-

Rone" and "Cla'ence," speaks about the relevance and importance of Black radio to the African-American community:

"Traditionally, Black radio has been the talking drum for the Black community. It gives voice to Black people who say: 'This is our opinion, our voice, our culture.' Ti-Rone (an 18-year syndicated advice show) is important because African Americans are not often asked their opinions to the degree whites are. So, in addition to being entertaining, Ti-Rone's response to listeners' letters and live street interviews help Blacks communicate, vent, and express their point of view in a format that's comfortable, relevant and informative," Sanders said.[98]

Radio is one of the most popular and efficient means for reaching African Americans frequently, at different times, and in a variety of locations.

During weekdays, before 8 A.M. and after 7 P.M., the majority of African Americans are more likely to listen to radio at home. However between those hours, a giant shift occurs, with more than 64 percent of the Black audience listening to the radio someplace outside their homes, according to Sanders.

African-American and urban-targeted radio formats reach more Black adults than any other format and rank high in all major radio metro areas. According to Arbitron's 2005 research edition of *Black Radio Today*, urban formats reach more than 45 percent of the 22 million African Americans ages 18 and older. In fact, with a 24 percent average quarter hour (AQH) share, Urban Contemporary is the favorite overall format of Blacks in the U.S., Urban Adult Contemporary (20 percent) is a close second, followed by Contemporary Hit Radio (13 percent). Religious formats (11 percent) also demonstrate notable strength among Black consumers, Sanders explained.

During an interview with Arbitron in 2004, Brian Knox, Senior Vice President/Director, Corporate Diversity for Katz Media Group talked about the importance and benefits of targeting African Americans via Urban radio. "Urban radio, specifically Black radio, is part of the cultural fabric of the Black community. Advertisers who want to send a clear-cut message that they want to do business within this community are able to extend a personalized invitation to Black Americans through the use of Urban radio. No other medium can extend this personalized invitation day in and day out the way Urban radio does."

Black Format Preferences

Black Persons 18–34

Format	Percent of Listeners
Urban Contemporary	60.8
Rhythmic/Contemporary Hit Radio	33.4
Urban Adult Contemporary	29.6
Pop Contemporary Hit Radio	22.3
Adult Contemporary	11.9

Black Persons 18–49

Format	Percent of Listeners
Urban Contemporary	51.0
Rhythmic/Contemporary Hit Radio	32.3
Urban Adult Contemporary	25.0
Pop Contemporary Hit Radio	16.2
Adult Contemporary	13.0

Black Persons 25–54

Format	Percent of Listeners
Urban Contemporary	43.0
Rhythmic/Contemporary Hit Radio	34.3
Urban Adult Contemporary	18.9
Pop Contemporary Hit Radio	15.5
Adult Contemporary	12.8

Black Persons 35+

Format	Percent of Listeners
Urban Contemporary	29.2
Rhythmic/Contemporary Hit Radio	28.1
Urban Adult Contemporary	15.5
Pop Contemporary Hit Radio	12.0
Adult Contemporary	10.9

Source: Scarborough USA, Release 1, 2003, 12 month data, © 2004 Arbitron Inc.

Black Listeners' Favorite Formats

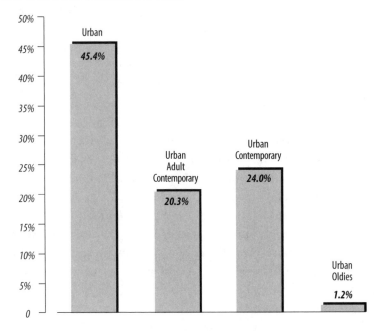

Television

At an average of 75.8 hours per week, African Americans watch 40 percent more TV than the general market. Despite their higher viewership ratings, many African-Americans complain about the lack of a variety of relevant programming needed to appeal to the different segments of the African-American population.

In a recent interview, Johnathan Rodgers, CEO of TV One, an African-American cable network, provides an explanation for television's impasse with regard to African-American programming: "Right or wrong, the general population will not necessarily support a drama about African-Americans, or even a sitcom. Sure, there are the *Fresh Prince* or *The Cosby Show*, but that is the exception rather than the rule."[99] Rodgers makes a good point. According to Nielsen Media Research, in the 2003–2004 television season, only *American Idol* and *NFL Monday Night Football* were in the Top 10 programs for both Blacks and whites.[100]

This isn't news. The ratings for the Top 10 rated primetime shows in African-American homes compared with white homes have differed significantly for years. The most glaring difference is that African Americans are watching "typical Black" shows—many of which are sitcoms that have been isolated to collectively run on a particular day on the UPN channel. For example, during the 2003–2004 season, Nielsen reported that UPN had six shows in the Top 10 for African Americans, none of which appeared in the Top 10 for whites.[101]

Rodgers also notes the valuable investment Blacks make in cable TV. "The largest portion of a Black family's investment in entertainment goes to the cable bill—almost $3 billion in total." The article highlights statistics from research conducted by the Cable Advertising Bureau showing that 78 percent of the 13.9 million Black TV households subscribe to cable, with 25 percent paying for digital services.[102]

This is significant as only a few cable providers are currently investing in shows that target African Americans. HBO and Showtime often feature movies, documentaries, and specials with a Black theme. Showtime gained a large number of subscribers when they premiered the *Soul Food* drama series, the only Black drama on television—network or cable —which ended its season in 2004.

TV One, a new cable network, is launching heavily Black-cast shows to provide an opportunity for African Americans to see themselves participating in venues such as poker, dating, and cooking—programs with long-standing appeal among white audiences. A couple of interesting culturally relevant make-over concepts include *Makeover Manor*, a Black makeover show that highlights and speaks directly to the hair care and skincare needs of Black women, and *Divine Makeover* which features the renovation of churches instead houses.

Print

Black print media is a major trusted source of information. Print media are considered the most established and responsible way to reach the African-American market, with more than 350 newspapers and magazines targeted at African Americans.

Seventy percent of African Americans read Black newspapers, and most will patronize businesses that advertise in these papers. African-American consumers also spend more time reading newspaper ads than do white consumers. In fact, 77.5 percent of African Americans seek product information in local papers, and 82.3 percent seek it in African-American magazines.

Additionally, there are over 150 African-American magazines.[103] Those with the largest readerships are *Ebony* (10.7 million), *Essence* (7.1 million), and *Black Enterprise* (4 million).

Credibility is given to Black media since they are from "our perspective" with information being trusted in newspapers by 79.7 percent, magazines by 87.0 percent.

African Americans and the Internet

According to the 2005 AOL African-American Cyberstudy conducted for AOL by Images Market Research, nearly 80 percent of African Americans have access to the internet versus 88 percent of the U.S. online population.[104] They have realized the most significant gains in usage during recent years compared with other races. As education and income levels increase, African Americans are spending more on computers and related equipment. Compared to whites, more African Americas are getting "wired" as younger surfers access the internet for a variety of purposes including entertainment (55 percent vs. 26 percent), health-related issues (72 percent vs. 53 percent), financial questions/needs (60 percent vs. 40 percent), and sports (39 percent vs. 26 percent).

African-Americans online:[105]

- Tend to be young and educated, with a penetration level for the college-educated comparable to that of whites at year-end 2003:

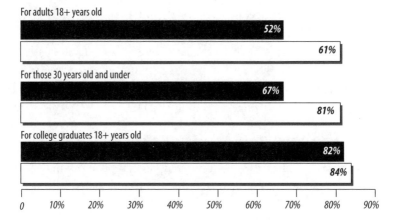

Internet Penetration by Category

- The average age of Blacks online is 36.6 years compared with 41.9 years for whites.

- Of those not currently online, 56 percent will eventually use the internet versus 35 percent of whites.

- Their purchases of computer and related equipment have increased 19 percent from $1.6 billion in 2000 to $1.9 billion in 2003.

- Among those African Americans who planned to attend a 4-year college in 2003, 94 percent had computer access at home and 50 percent owned their own computer, comparable with whites at 97 percent and 50 percent respectively.

- Blacks online are more likely to be from households with moderate to high incomes: 65 percent of those with household incomes of $50,000 or more were likely to go online in 2002 compared with 55 percent of those in the $20,000–$50,000 group, and 25 percent of those with household income of less than $20,000.

- According to the AOL Survey, Blacks are more likely to adopt new technologies and features faster than the general population; for example, two-thirds use broadband access compared with 53 percent of the general population.

- Those not using broadband are 27 percent more likely to acquire it in the next year than the general population, according to Digital Marketing Services (DMS).[106]

- Blacks are moderate users of the internet with an average of 44 hours being spent online per month, compared with 50 hours for whites, 42 sessions being logged and 1,186 pages being scanned.[115] They tend to read online advertisements and 46 percent find them informative compared with 26 percent of the general population, according to DMS.

Out-of-Home

Out-of-home advertising reaches and excites people where they live, work, play, and gather. "It is a media that is everywhere and when used with creativity, it creates brand new ad space where none existed—ad space that can stop people in their tracks," says EMC Outdoor, a specialist in outdoor media placement throughout the United States, Canada, Mexico, and South America, and Western Europe. Out-of-home media reaches its audiences in key ways with a simple direct message, and unlike TV, radio or print, out-of-home media cannot be turned off or put down.

Traditional vs. non-traditional formats

Traditionally, many marketers use 30- and 8-sheet billboard formats to reach African-American audiences. In fact, according to the Outdoor Advertising Association, billboards remain the cornerstone of outdoor media given their high-impact, strategic positioning, and market-to-market coverage. Eight sheet posters are often used in African-American communities to reach highly mobile African-American pedestrians as well as those in autos. Eight sheet primary out-of-home locations in the Black communities have been used in close proximity to retail outlets (near supermarkets, shopping centers and convenience stores). This makes sense given that shopping is one of the top three entertainment activities for most African Americans according to Yankelovich.

Up close and personal out-of-home formats like one-sheets, transit, and shelter ads also work well with African Americans because these formats have the ability to deliver tremendous stopping power. If the creative is executed in a manner that speaks to African-Americans' self-image, style, elegance and intellect, these formats deliver well on stopping power, eye-catching ability, and providing information in a relevant and convenient manner.

However, out-of-home has evolved beyond the traditional 30 and 8 sheet billboard. Just as other forms of media have had to evolve to accommodate a more segmented and mobile consumer market place, so to has out-of-home.

These expanded formats offer a more direct, intimate, in-your-face guerrilla marketing use of out-of-home as a medium. Some examples of the various formats are as follows:

- **Banners and wallscapes** can include target-specific messages on construction site buildings in and around Black communities.

- **Bus advertising** with target-specific messages on buses with routes that circulate in and around largely Black communities can be highly effective.

- **Cinema advertising** in movie complexes that feature urban films attract a captive audience of young Black moviegoers and have high ad recall rates.

- **Mobile billboards** can be driven directly to events and hard-to-reach locations within the Black community to celebrate events like Black History Month, and other special events indigenous to the African-American community.

- **Guerrilla marketing street teams** wearing poster jackets can interact directly with select African-American consumers, and hand out product and or literature to receptive passersby.

- **Taxi advertising** features lifestyle-relevant messages on cabs that arrive, circulate, and depart in and around areas where select African Americans congregate, i.e., clubs, bars, and restaurants.

- **Transit shelters** can target African-American pedestrians and vehicular traffic on heavily traveled streets within African-American communities.

- **Wrapped vehicles** make eye-catching displays that can be selected based on the normal driving pattern within African-American communities for a more focused event marketing strategy.

Both traditional and non-traditional formats are important for brand building and ultimately sales. Categories that have benefited from targeted African Americans via out-of-home include: retail and fashion, consumer goods, media and music, beverages, financial services, travel, telecommunications, healthcare, beauty products, utilities, special events, and public service.

Cost vs. other media

Given that 85 percent of African Americans live in metropolitan areas, specifically in central cities, out-of-home offers outstanding value and a variety of formats that can effectively reach the sizeable, increasingly mobile, and active African-American consumer market. On a cost per thousand comparison basis, out-of-home has always been seen as a relative good value by small budget advertisers, particularly those targeting the African-American consumer market. Even though most billboards and posters lack the recall attributes of sound and motion that other media have, if they are used strategically and tactically they can compliment other elements within the brand marketing mix to incrementally build familiarity and brand awareness. The following illustrates the general cost of various out-of-home formats versus other media:

Facts & Figures: CPM Comparison (2003)

	Men 18+	Women 18+	Adults
Outdoor (Top 50 Markets)			
8-Sheet Poster 350 Weekly GRPs	$1.77	$2.19	$0.98
30-Sheet Poster 350 Weekly GRPs	$2.61	$3.28	$1.45
Rotary Bulletin 70 Weekly GRPs	$6.72	$8.51	$3.76
Transit Shelter 350 Weekly GRPs	$2.07	$2.60	$1.15
Perm. Bulletin 70 Weekly GRPs	$7.88	$9.91	$4.39
Radio			
:30 network	$8.75	$7.75	—
:30 spot	$10.45	$9.65	—
Magazines			
Newsweeklies (4-color page)	$10.30	—	—
Newspapers			
Dailies (1/3 page black & white)	$22.05	$21.15	—
TV			
:30 prime-time network	$22.55	$18.10	—
:30 prime-time spot	$30.80	$24.31	—

Source: Media Dynamics, Inc. - TV Dimensions 2003 Telmar Outdoor Synergy

Proceed with caution

Despite the advantage of being cost-efficient, the size and number of billboards in Black communities have created an intrusive and persistent form of advertising. It is hard to avoid. For instance, a 1987 survey conducted by the city of St. Louis found twice as many billboards in Black neighborhoods as in white. Almost 60 percent of the billboards advertised cigarettes and alcoholic beverages. In another study of seventy-three billboards along nineteen blocks in a Black neighborhood in Philadelphia, sixty advertised cigarettes or alcohol. In fact, the Center for Disease Control estimates that billboards advertising tobacco products are placed in African-American communities four to five times more often in white communities. To that end, some African-American communities have responded to what seems to them to be a reckless disregard for social and public health issues in its communities.

Based on the product or message, marketers considering the use of out-of-home in the African-American community should be mindful of the following possibilities:

- Community backlash around the pervasive and disruptive clutter out-of-home creates

- A community that sees out-of-home as delivering messages that are detrimental to its social and public health concerns

- A medium that invades their communities and consciousness without their permission, and ability to turn it off or put it down.

Therefore, care must be taken with regards to the product selected and the message delivered when using out-of-home to target African Americans.

Word-of-Mouth

Word-of-mouth is central to brand building or brand erosion for any market segment. Within the African-American community, it is the most powerful non-traditional communication. Word-of-mouth is delivered and received across all African-American segments and its foundation is built upon four key elements: trust, respect, "open-voice," and "Black-to-Black" communication.

Trust and respect are the most important word-of-mouth characteristics. This is because it's important to be able to place confidence, belief, reliability, and responsibility in the person or organization delivering the message.

In a 1997 poll of Americans conducted by Guido H. Stempel III, young people, poor people, and African Americans were the most likely to believe in government conspiracy theories. However, due to the experience of racism and discrimination, popular conspiracy theories in the African-American community are usually not concocted stories, but are fueled by a racially sensitive event or an unfortunate episode in history that was racially motivated.

The term "open voice" refers to the ability to have an exchange of opinions that might not typically be heard or welcomed by the general population. It's feeling free to speak without censorship. The Black church, the only institution solely *owned* and *controlled* by the Black community, is an example of a vehicle that fosters open-voice communication. The traditional and cultural influence of the Black church provides the basis for African-American values. For many African Americans, the Black church serves as a resource for political, legal, and socio-economic directions as well as a social issues network. Dr. Melissa Harris-Lacewell, Assistant Professor of political science at the University of Chicago writes about the influence of the attitudes and opinions in the Black church in her book *Barbershops, Bibles and BET: Everyday Talk and Black Political Thought:* "In Black communities, the church is a critical location for the definition of truth, and as individuals interact with one another and with church leadership, they enter a process that helps them create a worldview."

"Black-to-Black" communication is similar to "open voice" except that ideas and messages are communicated exclusively between African Americans. An example would be the conversations held in Black-owned, operated, and frequented beauty salons and barbershops. According to Segmented Marketing Services Inc., (SMSi) African-American women spend 2 to 4 hours at the beauty salon per visit—twice as long on average as general market clients. And for generations, African-American men have congregated in the barbershops to share news and information. According to an interview conducted with Dr. Harris-Lacewell by the *Chicago Tribune,* (April 20, 2004) "The barbershop is yet another forum where political ideas take shape. The back and forth debate and fluid discourse reveal the deep divergence in Black perspective not often captured by traditional research." And not often captured by traditional media. Thus, these businesses have, for years, provided an important communication outlet for the African-American community and contribute immensely to the word-of-mouth process.

Street Credit: The New Word-of-Mouth

In addition to street cool, another influencing factor derived from Black men in the African-American community is "street credibility," an off-shoot of street cool.

We have heard several points-of-view from Black men on how this attitude is displayed, but most will agree it's all about having street status and influence. For many Black men, street credit is an outgrowth from the need for them to earn respect, if not from America, then from their peers. For marketers, street credibility is another powerful form of word-of-mouth that translates to believability and authenticity.

Brandon Miller, a 24-year-old freelance journalist in Washington, D.C., and the epitome of hip-hop style who sports braids, baggy jeans, and oversized shirts, defines street credibility this way: "Street cred is about having respect from your peers. It's macho, machismo, being down (to earth), and having a rep that precedes a person; a rep that says this person accomplished something. This could be anything from being a ladies man, a streetwise thug, or a hustler trying to make money, legally."

Adrian Bond, a thirty-something software technician from Dallas is the antithesis in appearance from Mr. Miller. He sports a contemporary style of close-cropped twists, relaxed fit designer jeans, and Kenneth Cole boots. He echoes Mr. Miller's point of view and adds, "Street credit is important. It's about being recognized and respected by our own people. It's about first impressions, how you look and having influence." Interestingly, both Miller and Bond agree that they have a certain amount of street credit within their peer group.

Street credit's mass appeal is also evident by the following illustrations:

- Street credibility and notorious rapper, Snoop Dogg, is what gave Tangueray its phenomenal sales after Snoop mentioned the brand in his "Gin and Juice" video.

- Although Bill Cosby can be credited with some early exposure of Australia's Coogi sweaters when he sported a few on *The Cosby Show*, it was the street credibility from rappers that helped the company enjoy unparalleled sales and awareness.

- At this writing, McDonald's has engaged the services of an enter-tainment-marketing firm in a move to get hip-hop artists to begin dropping the name of the company's Big Mac into rhymes.

Grass Roots

Grass roots marketing is like being able to look your consumer in the eye and tell them something personal.
—Ron Campbell, President, Campbell Communications

Grass roots marketing is a powerful and underused method for reaching African-American consumers. Although many corporations have made great strides to reach African-American consumers through this up-close-and-personal method, many are still hesitant about permeating the Black community with their messages and presence.

Research studies reveal that African Americans respond more favorably to brands and companies that support their communities, not only with their dollars, but also with their presence. These consumers expect a long-term commitment beyond "a banner and booth."

Following are some grass roots methods that have a high success rate with the African-American community.

Affinity Marketing

Simply put, affinity marketing is the building and use of partnerships. Affinity marketing is a collaborative marketing effort between two or more companies in order to acquire or retain customers. In today's environment where budgets are being cut and marketers are looking for ways to reach customers to get a better return on their marketing investment, affinity-marketing approaches have become increasingly popular. In such cases, costs are reduced, new channels to the consumer are opened, and complimentary brands can attract responses from the consumer that neither party could attract on its own.

In the Black community we are seeing an increase in the number of authorized strategic alliances between companies attempting to build awareness, expand their customer bases, create buzz, or enhance their brand images among various segments within the community. The best places to look for affinity partners to build trust with Black consumers continue to be some of the following:

- Non-profit organizations within the Black community such as
  The National Urban League, 100 Black Men of America, and
  African-American cultural institutions.

- Minority business seminars such as *Black Enterprise*'s Entrepreneurial Conferences and the *Black Enterprise* Golf and Tennis
  Challenge

- Black music events such as the *Essence* Music Festival and *Vibe*
  Music Fest, and sporting events at Historically Black Colleges and
  Universities.

Provide a Hand Up, Not a Hand Out

In 2003, Wells Fargo Bank presented an innovative free seminar in California to assist African Americans in understanding strategies to build
wealth with concentrations on real estate, saving and investing, and
entrepreneurship. In 2004 additional seminars were added in Texas and
Maryland. Wells Fargo partnered with Kelvin Boston,
motivational speaker and author of "Smart Money
Moves for African Americans," Gail Perry-Mason
author of "Girl, Make Your Money Grow," and entrepreneur Stedman Graham who also authored, "You
Can Make It Happen." The first daylong seminar
attracted 300 African Americans and since then the seminars have
attracted more than 2,000 attendees. The relevant speakers and work-
shop directors were positive role models who made the learning process
interesting and fun!

> **Wells Fargo's financial seminars for African Americans resulted in 300 new customers**

According to Cheryl McDonald, Wells Fargo's African-American Segment Manager, the seminars have been very successful for the attendees
and Wells Fargo. "From the seminars, the mortgage concept has taken
off well outside of the bank," states McDonald. She further explains,
"From the attendance of one event alone, we closed 100 home loans. At
another event where we had participation from 1,000 attendees, Wells
Fargo gained 300 new customers."

You can do well by doing good

Choosing the right affinity partner when targeting the Black community can be both cost effective and a way for marketers to build trust

and establish residual goodwill. Partnership programs with influential organizations, groups, and institutions that have the trust of the Black community have historically helped position marketers in categories like alcoholic beverages and tobacco to avoid being perceived as carpetbaggers who exploit Black youth. A successful example of this kind of affinity effort is the Perspective In African American Art program, a 10-year collaboration with Seagram's Gin, which started with the National Urban League, and later expanded to six African-American cultural institutions in Atlanta, Chicago, Dallas, Detroit, Los Angles, and New York in celebration of Black History Month.

This strategic alliance allowed Seagram's Gin to establish its support of contemporary African-American art and culture by introducing a program to foster African-American artistic expression. Over the years the program has presented each institution with a grant for the development of a Community in Residence Program. Each year, an emerging African-American artist from each of the six regions is commissioned to create a work of art that celebrated the African-American experience. During the Black History month celebration at each institution the artist's work is unveiled. Invitations to attend the unveiling are extended to community influencers and promoted in and covered by Black media. This collaboration is a "win-win" for all parties involved. Seagram's Gin is positioned as being supportive and as giving something back to the Black community, and the National Urban League, and the six cultural institutions receive funds needed to sustain themselves as nonprofit institutions.

Hip-hop Gets Down with the Deals
—*Business Week Online* article headline, May 18, 2005

Hip-hop artists have long paid homage to brands from Cadillac to Cartier without "getting paid" and cashing in on the rewards of the hip-hop culture. David Kiley of *BusinessWeek Online* states that "musicians of an earlier generation used to sneer at corporate sponsorships. For today's stars such sponsorships are cool and lucrative."

The influence of hip-hop stems from its crossover popularity in suburbs, in addition to its obvious domination in urban markets, making strategic alliances with hip hop artists more popular than ever. Major artists like Ludacris, Big Boi, and Jermaine Dupri are even proactively meeting with major ad agencies to tell marketing executives what kind of collaborative sponsorships and deals would interest them. This is a major shift in mind set. Hip-hop artists who have extended their brands without being labeled sell-outs usually have done so by staying true to their hip-hop lifestyles with products that carry a certain cachet or boast "bling." Consider these examples:

- The collaboration between Russell Simmons' Phat Farm brand, a leader in classic urban fashion, and Motorola, a leading global cell-phone manufacturer, to market a special designer cell phone targeting young style-conscious urban youth.

- The partnership of hip-hop rapper Jay Z and expensive watch-maker Audemarts Piguet to market a luxury watch that will be priced to personify the ultimate "bling."

- Antwan "Big Boi" Patton of Outkast reaped a six-figure deal in 2003 after he recorded *Hey Ya!,* which featured the recurring line, "Shake it like a Polaroid picture." The deal included appearing in ads and performing with product in hand.

Perhaps no artist is better at managing this collaborative alliance than the rap artist 50 Cent. With three of the top 10 songs on the Billboard Hot 100 list, 50 Cent has his own line of hot-selling Reebok International shoes and apparel, which has surpassed Reebok sales for any NBA star and for rival artist Jay Z. The deal calls for 50 Cent to help develop products, perform in ads, and wear the clothes and shoes in performances and videos. Reebok, meanwhile, is cross–promoting 50 Cent's music.

"The only boundary the artist and advertiser are looking for is that it feels authentic and not scripted," says Lori Senecal, director of agency McCann-Erickson's youth marketing unit.

New York marketing consultant Mastermind Group estimates that there are 100 million consumers worldwide who buy music with what is called the "urban mindset," with lyrics about city life, sex, violence, sports, and brand worship. That is a bigger market than the U.S. Baby Boom generation.

The best kinds of affinity partners are those who haven't previously participated in similar alliances. Finding a celebrity or an organization that has never been involved in co-marketing a product ensures that you will maximize the trust that you generate, and minimize the confusion of which product is associated with them. The astute affinity marketer will find an unaffiliated partner that inhabits the same niche his product does.

Buzz Marketing

Word-of-mouth marketing isn't about you and your brand. It's about them—the people who will start the conversation for you.
                                             —Mark Hughes, *Buzzmarketing*

There is a difference between *buzz* and *buzz marketing*. *Buzz* has been around for as long as people have shared ideas. It is the word-of-mouth effect, the transfer of information through social networks. And it can happen spontaneously, without a nudge from a marketer or anyone else. *Buzz marketing*, on the other hand, is the scripted use of action to generate *buzz*. It is deliberate. One of the factors that sets buzz marketing apart from other forms of marketing is the illusion of spontaneity, the invisibility of the marketer.

The slightly subversive, slightly underground technique that forms the basis of buzz marketing has been building in popularity for a few years. But now a convergence of factors has helped to make buzz marketing more attractive than ever. For one thing buzz is cheap. There are no national media buys and no expensive creative components, and the rise of the internet means marketers can reach just about anyone in almost any semblance they care to assume.

Additionally, buzz marketing attempts to make each encounter with a consumer look like a unique, serendipitous event. Authenticity is the key. This is uniquely appealing to the desirable urban African-American "twentysomething" trendsetters who remain skeptical of traditional mass advertising.

Buzz marketing arms these young urban African-American "twenty-somethings" with tools or knowledge they can take back to their peer groups so they will be perceived as being "in the know." Mark Hughes, author of *Buzzmarketing* (Penguin/Portfolio, 2004–2005) says you have to be a "buzz giver"—creating a readymade story to make the twentysomethings the center of interest. Ultimately the marketer's brand benefits because an accepted member of the social circle will always be more credible than any communication that comes directly from the brand.

Building a successful buzz campaign hinges on finding the right carrier for the message—influencers who are obsessed with staying one step ahead of their peers. Malcolm Gladwell, in his book, *The Tipping Point: How Little Things Can Make a Big Difference,* says "the right ones . . . can turn a grass fire into a conflagration." In other words, "they can make it hot." The goal in the Black community is to seek out the trendsetters and subtly push them into talking up your brand to their friends and admirers.

Youth in America's inner cities, with their extraordinary peer pressure network generate tremendous word-of-mouth. Currently the "right trendsetting carriers," the ones with the most "street credibility" are the hip-hoppers, with all other demographic, ethnic, and cultural groups gradually following.

Among these young trendsetting carriers the kinds of products that seem to generate the most buzz are "observable products" such as clothes, cars, cellular phones, video games, alcoholic beverages, music videos, and movies. People tend to talk about things they see, particularly in the Black community where products become visible status symbols or obtain "badge" value status.

Technology is accelerating word-of-mouth. Andrea Fant-Hobbs, Senior Vice-President, Account Director at Vigilante, a multicultural advertising firm, recognizes the importance of grassroots efforts, but has observed how many marketers overlook opportunities to use these efforts with current technology.

Accordingly, Fant-Hobbs also believes the name is dated. "When I hear grass roots, I think of antiquated methods like 'papering places' or going to an organization and setting up a booth. Not that any of these are wrong, but when I think about the emergence of technology, Palm Pilots, phones that take pictures, the question becomes, 'How can we reach the Black consumer in a more engaging way?' A better name for grass roots is 'buzz marketing' because today it's really about connecting people to marketing, media, and PR and getting the brand at the top of the list and in the face of consumers."

Historical practitioners of buzz marketing in the African-American community include alcohol and tobacco advertisers. Long excluded from mass media, they have an obvious interest in making any sort of buzz work. They have become adept at making their products familiar through targeted cultural marketing strategies. Sometimes the aggressive and questionable marketing practices designed to appeal to young inner city African Americans draw the ire of the Black community. Keep in mind that the African-American community is socially active, and as a result it responds when there seems to be a reckless disregard for social and public health issues in its communities. Marketing campaigns that encourage the consumption of alcohol and tobacco among young African-American adults and youth have often been deemed a "no-no" and subject to generating major "negative" buzz.

One caution on word-of-mouth: It may spread more negative comments to people than it does positive ones. To minimize the risk of negative reaction, marketers should be motivated to contribute, rather than simply exploit, when targeting the African-American community.

Guerrilla Marketing

With guerrilla marketing the focus changes from the volume of advertising to the impact of the message
—Conrad Levinson, *The Handbook of Guerrilla Marketing*

Guerrilla marketing is another progression of buzz marketing. It is part of a growing sector of marketing that foregoes traditional creative efforts and media buys in favor of inexpensive, in-your-face tactics that take advertisers messages directly to the consumer—very directly. Unlike word-of-mouth buzz marketing, there is nothing subtle about it. In fact, other than a piece of direct mail, guerrilla marketing is the ultimate way to get into the face of people so that they cannot get away from the message targeting them.

It is also a good way to cut costs. Guerrilla marketing came about as a means for companies to cheaply undercut competitors' marketing efforts, said Peter Shih, an executive vice president of marketing and communications at the American Advertising Federation, based in Washington, D.C.

"Guerrilla marketing started about 20 years ago from sports marketing," Shih said. "What would happen is somebody would spend a lot of money to sponsor events, and someone else would figure out how to do it on the cheap. During the Olympic Games you had one sneaker company who was the major sponsor and another who set up billboards around the whole place and was giving away its merchandise to some of the athletes. If you are talking about $20 million or $35 million in sponsorship rights, that's a lot of money to save." he said.

Today, in the black community the practice of guerrilla marketing is best executed through specialty agencies whose expertise is generating buzz among trendsetting influencers in major urban markets like New York, Atlanta, Chicago, Los Angles, and Oakland. They promote and provide organized "street teams" of influential trendsetters for guerrilla marketing.

Recently we have observed that some companies who are up against more established, heavier spending, and better-known, brand name competitors shy away from more traditional marketing media such as television, radio, and print and instead use word-of-mouth to build awareness and spread their names.

A recent example is Brooklyn Xpress, a modestly priced urban apparel line that is trying to crack the New York market through a grass roots campaign. Unable to compete with established players like Rocawear, Ecko Unlimited, and Fubu that boast big hip-hop names and even bigger ad budgets, the company is banking on word-of-mouth to spread its name.

In seeking to generate buzz, the company hired Ambient Planet, an urban specialty marketing firm, to provide "street teams" to give away thousands of shirts, hats, and other apparel items at more than a dozen New York high schools in the hope of building brand awareness. "Our program is just to reach out to these schools and make customers aware of who we are and what we are about" said Jay Schwartz, vice president of Brooklyn Xpress.

Brooklyn Xpress isn't the first to try a novel approach. A growing number of marketers are seeking to generate buzz by hiring "street teams" for guerrilla marketing. Some even recruit high school students to act as influential trendsetters in the belief that they gain unprecedented access to students on their home ground.

Product Sampling

Lafayette and Sandy Jones, owners of Segmented Marketing Services (SMSi) a retail merchandising, marketing, and publishing company in Winston-Salem, North Carolina, are committed to grass roots marketing and, in fact, have built a profitable business around their huge sampling resource network. The Joneses believe, "Trial is everything!" SMSi distributes 100 million free product samples a year to African Americans and Latinos via their numerous community networking resources including: churches, beauty and barbershops, and neighborhood and campus events. During an interview, Lafayette and Sandy Jones provided their expertise and insights about product sampling among African-American consumers.

According to the Joneses, "Retailers have learned that sampling can increase sales by 40 percent. No other component of a marketing plan even comes close to its effectiveness." Product sampling among African-American consumers provides a huge opportunity for marketers because it is welcomed and seen as "different" for these consumers. According to SMSi fewer than 5 percent of African Americans receive samples. "Thus," according to Sandy Jones, "many welcome these products as they view them as a gift rather than as an entitlement. The best way to reach the ethnic customer is to find places where they live work, play shop, worship, and groom."

SMSi says the community network or non-traditional sampling is effective because:

- It is done through the "gatekeepers"—people whom African Americans trust—the minister, hairstylists, barber, etc. This makes for automatic implied endorsement.

- Many African Americans dwell in multiple-family households (60 percent) and are not in the typical marketing database. Many also share a common mailbox.

- Approximately 40 percent of African Americans do not use traditional banking services (credit cards, checking accounts), according to the American Bankers Association) which means they often are not included in direct mail databases.

- African Americans are more likely to have an unlisted phone number.

- Many African Americans use post office mailboxes as a safe, reliable means for getting their mail because they may be highly transient or because they have started a business.

As a result of network sampling, SMSi also reports that the conversion from sample to full size and full price is higher among African Americans than the general population.

In a study with independent market research firm Johnson and Associates of Chicago, SMSi used the Church Family Network to provide samples of soft drink products to 3.1 million African-American and Latino families in 8,000 churches. Conversion to full-size purchase after using a sample showed conversion results as high as 90 percent for African Americans who bought full-size diet-soda products. According to Deborah Johnson-Hall, president of the firm, "Our business is ethnic research and seldom do we see trial or conversion at such levels among ethnic consumers."

"There's no doubt about it. Ethnic sampling creates trial and trial is the best way to achieve future product purchases among ethnic shoppers," says Lafayette Jones.[107]

Marketing in a New Age

The three new roles for advertising are: to empower, to demonstrate, and to involve.
—Joseph Jaffe in *Life After the 30-Second Spot,* an Adweek Book

As marketers continue to look for ways to reach consumers and get a better return for their money they have become increasingly willing to experiment with non-traditional forms of marketing. The array of traditional marketing tools that leans heavily on the standard 30-second commercial is being questioned.

As an example, according to *BusinessWeek,* "In 2004, McDonald's devoted one-third of its U.S. marketing budget to television, compared with two-thirds five years prior. Money that used to go for 30-second network spots now pays for closed circuit sports programming piped into Latino bars, and for ads in *Upscale,* a custom-published magazine distributed to Black barbershops. To sharpen its appeal to young men, another of its prime-target audiences, McDonald's advertises on Foot

Locker Inc.'s in-store video network. The company zeroes in on mothers through ads in women's magazines such as *O: The Oprah Magazine*, and *Marie Claire* and on websites like Yahoo and iVillage Inc." Today, says *BusinessWeek* in the same article, it is easier to send the right message to your target audience by using the available array of narrowcast electronic channels, specialized magazines, and websites.[108]

African Americans have been early adopters of these new channels of communication, which offer marketers the ability to target and deliver more culturally relevant content and messaging to Black consumers than can readily be done through mass media. This becomes increasingly important as marketers evolve out of the "one size fits all" approach to marketing and are able to act upon the age, economic, social, gender, class, and generational distinctions found within today's African-American consumer market.

New marketing approaches, some based on the use of new technology that allows African-American consumers more engaging experiences on all the devices with which they interact include:

- **The internet** where the rise of high speed connections is making the internet much more compelling to young trendsetting African-American consumers. AOL BlackVoices is an example of a targeted website that offers advertisers the added opportunity to reach and engage African-American consumers with flashier ads enlivened by video, audio, animation, and greater interactivity. (See more on internet use among African Americans on page 65.)

- **Video games and services** where African Americans, according to a Nielsen Entertainment benchmark study, reported spending more money than any other demographic group. Gaming also offers marketers a medium that leverages sight, sound, motion, and interactivity with the added value of reaching these consumers where they want to be reached and without interruption. Gaming has surpassed much of today's available content to bring forth a film- or television-like experience that is being consumed by people who concede that it's no fun playing alone, unlike watching television which is often done alone.

- **Experiential marketing** is a higher level of event marketing. It is the non-technological or offline expression of the ability to involve, to offer consumers a tangible and sustainable experience. An excellent example of experiential marketing is Ford Motor Company's Lincoln Mark LT brand teaming up with NBA legend Earvin "Magic" Johnson. This pairing takes advantage of the trend toward personalization and highlights ways that the Mark LT can be customized. The event and ad campaign, developed and executed by Uniworld Group, was launched in the summer of 2005. It featured events in Los Angeles; Washington, D.C.; and Miami; and culminated with an on-line auction to benefit the Magic Johnson Foundation, which further involves Lincoln Mark LT's customers. According to Ed Boyd, group account director for Uniworld, "This effort shows that the brand is interested in the African-American market. Importantly, African Americans tend to appreciate this type of high-quality effort because they have had a long-standing belief that they are being taken for granted."

• **Interactive ads** have started to click on cable and satellite TV. When Sony launched a television ad for its action movie *XXX: State of the Union* in April 2005, Echo-Star Communication Corporation's satellite television subscribers got more than 30 seconds of explosions and fistfights. An icon appeared on the screen inviting viewers to push a button on their remote if they wanted to learn more about the film. Doing so switched them to a 30-minute program giving more details on the movie as well as interviews with stars Samuel Jackson and Ice Cube. It even included the first 10 minutes of the movie. Other advertisers are also sticking their toes into the water in the belief that this new technology will let viewers use TV ads to seek out information and even order specific products much as consumers today use websites.

What all these new approaches have in common is they may be a provocative way for advertisers and marketers to re-engage with African-American consumers and continue to transform and build brands.

EIGHT

Best Practice Activities Are Required to Succeed in Marketing to African Americans

Follow the same principles as in the general market, understand these consumers and market consistently, not just on Martin Luther King Jr.'s birthday.

—Howard Buford, CEO of Prime Access,
specialist in multicultural advertising

As most successful marketers recognize the business opportunity in catering to and targeting the specific needs of African-American consumers, they also learn that unless undertaken in the right way, the results can be disappointing. The keys to success in marketing to the African-American market are pretty much the same as those of any successful business venture:

- Start with senior management and fully agree as an organization and commit to the African-American segment as a compatible-brand, business-building opportunity.

- Build a marketing plan with realistic objectives based on targeted insights that provide an in-depth understanding of the African-American consumer.

- Authorize realistic budgets that reflect the necessary spending or funding based on the competitive environment of the market and the projected share of market goals.

- Incorporate local advertising and relationship marketing to generate visibility, respect, and legitimacy for the brand.

- Use outside resources to ensure authenticity.

- Don't dabble, stay committed, market consistently, be patient, and remember, "Rome wasn't built in a day."

Organization Support

Senior Management "Buy-In"

Senior management attention and central direction is needed to prevent African-American marketing from becoming an afterthought. The most important action is to obtain "buy-in" from senior management that the African-American consumer market is a growth opportunity and is consistent with the business strategy and capabilities of the company.

While working on the Black consumer market business for the first time, Freddie Clary, Associate Director of Advertising Research for Time Inc. spoke about the importance of organizational commitment and senior management buy-in when targeting this segment: "It's hard to get middle-management-level people to make changes. It takes commitment throughout the entire organization. Kraft and Proctor & Gamble are good models. They don't have to start from scratch in that they are trying to understand what's important to African-American consumers across all their efforts. At *Essence*, [for example] we advocate for Black women and we have people involved at a higher level. That's new to me. It's a whole different feeling."

The process starts with getting a concise, insightful, and comprehensive analysis of the marketplace and the marketer's organization. This initiative will provide a quantitative and qualitative decision-making base for the strategic rationale to secure the necessary fiscal commitment to the African-American market as a viable growth opportunity. You need to know the following:

- Size of opportunity
- "Fit" with company capabilities
- Consistency with brand and company image
- Existing relationship with intended target audience
- Resource capability
- Competition
- Opportunity gaps
- Expected return on investment
- Brand-building capabilities

- Strength of current product line
- Benefit capability of current product line to the targeted consumer

Gathering and Evaluating Information

Target market definition and segmentation is the most important step in preparing a business review. Effective marketing to the African-American market is impossible without a thorough understanding of this customer base. Keeping cultural insights and differences more top-of-mind can lead to valuable opportunities. This step requires a commitment to, and an investment in, relevant research.

Investment in research and analysis alone is not enough. It is important to remember that African-American consumer data does not always equal African-American consumer insights. "Relevant research" is research that is executed in a very thoughtful and target-specific manner (such as a quantitative survey combined with ethnographies) that provides actionable, strategic insights that are shared throughout the organization.

Commit to Adequate Marketing Spending

Authorize realistic budgets that reflect the necessary spending and funding based on a category's competitive environment and projected share of market goals.

While marketers are allocating more marketing budgets to multicultural segments, their investments remain very low given the growth with the African-American population and their spending power. The average ad budget of respondents who participated in the 2004 Association of National Advertisers (ANA) survey was $225 million, with just $4.8 million devoted to all multicultural efforts. This represents a little more than 2 percent against an emerging consumer segment that represents nearly 30 percent of the population. Even more interesting, 54 percent of respondents to the ANA survey said that their ad budgets remained the same compared with the prior year.[109]

The picture is further complicated by the growing preference for marketing to Latinos based on their 59 percent population-growth spurt from 1990 to 2000.[110] This preference has come primarily at the expense of the African-American market as many companies are shifting dollars from African-American ad budgets to the Latino market. Cheryl May-berry McKissack, CEO of Nia Enterprises explains, "They took dollars typically in one multicultural pot and divided them up." This could be viewed as the modern day equivalent of "robbing from Peter to pay Paul" only in this case it is, "robbing from Malik to pay Juan."

The problem with this scenario is that, aside from pitting the individual market segments against each other for funding, it continues the ill-conceived practice of marginalization and under-investment in both ethnic consumer segments, with regard to their current and future pay-out potential and projected ROI.

Improve Target-Market Execution

In addition to national efforts, incorporate local advertising and relationship marketing to generate visibility, respect, and legitimacy for the brand. Improving the execution of marketing to the African-American market requires the undertaking of more complex, regionally oriented marketing activities.

Relationship marketing that increases the visibility of the brand and company and brings the product or service in direct contact with the targeted consumer has proven to be an extremely effective marketing tool within the African-American community. Relationship marketing has been particularly effective in demonstrating how a product or service can enhance the distinct social and cultural lifestyle choices of African Americans.

When synergistically and strategically integrated into the brand budget and marketing plan process, relationship marketing can provide an opportunity to dramatically increase brand ROI. The message can be personalized and custom tailored to the unique needs of this consumer segment to build brand trial, brand retention, and brand loyalty.

Historically, companies like Ford, McDonald's, General Motors, Sears, and AT&T have increased market share while earning kudos for their continuous visibility, activity, and support of programs that are important to the African-American community. More recently companies like Verizon and Bank of America have recognized the importance of establishing a culturally relevant relationship while marketing to African Americans. The Chicago Symphony Orchestra reached out to numerous local African-American affinity groups and events to spread the word about its targeted and well-received Classical Tapestry Series.

Use External Resources

Use outside resources to ensure authenticity. The advantages of using an advertising agency or marketing firm that specializes in the African-American consumer are:

- Access to invaluable ethnic insights.

- Ability to adapt positioning and accurately target the message.

- Execution of marketing programs and campaigns that reach the ethnic consumer efficiently.

- An African-American focused specialty agency is better equipped to provide authenticity and expertise. This seems to be confirmed by the *2004 ANA Multicultural Marketing Study* in which 85 percent of marketers said they used a multicultural agency—up from 76 percent in 2002.

The consensus seems to be that ethnic-focused agencies add the most value through these distinct offerings:

- Minority ownership and diversity in staff who better understand and empathize with the targeted consumer;

- Ability to add depth to ethnic insights;

- Local community knowledge and access;

- African-American media connections;

- Assistance in overcoming barriers to relationships across racial lines, and;

- Language skills for accurate translations.

Partnering with African-American specialty agencies can best mitigate the challenges and risks inherent in marketing to Black consumers. This is especially true when the specialty agency is involved in overall planning for the brand at the initial strategy development stage, and not expected to develop the ethnic strategy as an afterthought once the overall strategy is locked in.

NINE

Conducting Research with Relevance and Insight

Research, of course, at its best contributes to both understanding and creativity. The best research is not only revealing; it's stimulating and provocative.
— Susan Gianinno, Chairman and CEO, Publicis[111]

As cultural differences require different marketing approaches for African Americans compared with the general population, the same statement also applies to marketing research.

When conducting research among the African-American segment, The Hunter-Miller Group follows industry standards and uses traditional designs and methods, carefully noting along the way, what works and what doesn't. What we have learned over the years is that the outcome of the research often depends on how African Americans are approached and how "comfortable" they feel in a research setting.

Qualitative settings have been instrumental in helping clients understand what makes African Americans tick by establishing a dialogue with them. However, during these settings we have also observed that many African Americans have a higher propensity than some whites to be politically correct—responding with what they think others want to hear. Many shy away from "embracing their own Blackness" by putting on the "white face" even when they're among all Black participants.

What many African Americans feel in their hearts sometimes differs from the intellectual process they go through before they respond within a research framework. For example, in qualitative sessions where automobiles are the focus, what African Americans *feel* and what they *say* about the importance of automobile ownership differs.

What African Americans **Feel** is important in vehicle selection:	What African Americans **Say** is important in vehicle selection:
Style	Performance
Luxury	Safety
Comfort	Fuel Economy
Ability to attract attention	Value

As mentioned earlier, to many African Americans, automobiles have tremendous badge value. For those who will never purchase a home, a car is the largest, most important purchase in their lives. It becomes a material representation of who they are. However, the need to fit in, to please, and to be included is often the motivator behind some of the responses in Black groups. This is not to say that marketers should avoid conducting qualitative research with African Americans, but rather they should consider the impact of cultural nuances with regard to the research approach and develop studies and exercises with these distinctions and behavior patterns in mind.

Getting the Most from African-American Respondents

Following are some suggestions and illustrations of different approaches and examples that required a different design when planning and conducting research among the African-American segment.

Identify the Target and the Market

While quantitative information about African Americans is increasing, there continues to be limited information about African-American consumers outside of proprietary studies. For the marketer with little or no experience with African Americans, we suggest the following checklist of options as a place to start:

- **Use Census data to help identify, define, or create a rationale for your target.**
- **Use brand and category development indices (BDI and CDI)** and other syndicated research information to identify consumer brand and category use.
- **Conduct quantitative research in areas of awareness and usage (including competitors).**

- **Conduct qualitative research to establish a dialogue with the target.**

- **Use BDI and CDI to select markets.** Consider markets with high concentrations of African Americans and research facilities that are experienced and accessible to this target.

- **Modify "by-the-book" methods. Relax the qualifiers.** In many cases, a general market study will precede an African-American study and will be used as the model for the design of the African-American study. Too often, however, general market specifications and methodologies don't fit the real world situations of the African-American target.

- **Employ the "buddy system." Relax the affinity clause (bring a friend).** While companies conduct more research among the African-American market than 20 years ago, we have found that many African Americans, even the most sophisticated, have not been exposed to the market research experience. Moreover, first time "virgin" respondents may be skeptical about the process. Depending on the study, whether a tough recruit, informal exploratory conversations, or where heightened sensitivities might be apparent, establishing and increasing the comfort level becomes significant. By relaxing the affinity clause for focus groups, for example, and allowing a friend to participate in the same group (provided they meet all other stipulated screening criteria) we have noticed that, as the comfort level increases, so does the flow of conversation and the amount of valuable information.

- **Change the environment.** While trying to better develop a special program to help children from high-risk environments feel safe, Children's Memorial Hospital in Chicago requested a series of focus groups among mothers who were residents of public housing. Instead of conducting the interviews at a typical focus group facility, where the atmosphere might prohibit them from speaking honestly about their environment and challenges within their lifestyle, groups were conducted in a vacant apartment within the public housing community. One room served as the group room where respondents were audio and videotaped. Another room was set up for client viewing via a TV monitor.

The 95 percent show rate complemented the excellent discussions. Respondents indicated that they felt valued and were appreciative of the fact that we met with them on their turf. Ethnographies and in-home interviews are important research methodologies that also work well with African-Americans. Respondents' natural environments foster a comfort level that contributes to honest, straightforward, thoughtful responses.

- **Use thought-provoking questions that don't alienate.** From a quantitative standpoint, prior research has shown that African Americans have a tendency to rate highly those issues, concepts, ideas, and services that have a positive effect on the community. Shorebank is a white-owned financial services institution that serves the African-American community via retail branches. Shorebank is a major player in community development, investing millions in property renovation and small business loans. When Shorebank requested a customer satisfaction survey to measure the effectiveness of its services among targeted customers who are primarily Boomers and Matures, many African Americans rated the bank's services with high scores to the point where learning was limited. This was not to say that African Americans weren't being honest, but a couple of things were happening:

  Compared with the general market, African Americans feel that they are not often asked for their opinion. Therefore, it is not uncommon to see a trend of contrasting extremes especially with regard to issues and situations affecting the community.

  There is a history and perception among African Americans that "good things get taken away; bad things are here to stay" (particularly among Boomers and Matures). Not surprisingly, follow-up focus groups with customers revealed that Shorebank's African-American customers wanted to ensure that the community programs were not taken away, or changed for the worse.

- **Invite African-American participants to be Black.** In qualitative settings, it's not enough to have an African-American moderator conduct a group with all Black respondents. While this scenario is important, and basic to African-American qualitative research, we have observed that many African Americans in focus group settings continue to hold back. Having "lived Black" for many years (i.e., living, socializing, and worshiping in pre-dominately Black communities) our objective in the focus group setting is always to obtain that cocktail, "round the kitchen table" chatter that African Americans often have with family and friends. However, as respondents are exiting the focus group room, we sometimes hear, "Why the all-Black group?" or "I wanted to say 'X.' but didn't want to embarrass you or my brothers and sisters in the group." And it dawned on us that they were uncomfortable being Black in this setting.

During her presentation at the Advertising Research Foundation's 49th Annual Conference in 2003 entitled *Amazingly Relevant Research*, Susan Gianinno spoke about the importance of conducting relevant research and "disarming respondents into revealing their truths." Even before we were exposed to Ms. Gianinno's speech, we began disarming African-American respondents by inviting them to share their opinions from an African-American perspective "as needed" or "as the spirit moves them." Today, we introduce a simple invitation, to wear their consumer hats and their African-American hats, and the results have proven to be monumental in tearing down the wall of uncertainty and discomfort with African-American respondents.

- **Disarm African-American respondents: Help them uncover "their truth."** Another example, of disarming African-American respondents comes from a qualitative study for a nationwide mortgage company. All of the 40 African-American respondents declared that race was not a criterion when selecting a mortgage officer. However, when equal numbers of headshot photographs of younger and older, white and Black, business-attired males and females were presented to the respondents to select one person with whom they would like to do business (all criteria being equal) 39 of 40 choose a photo of an African-American. Respondents were even surprised by their own choices. Then the truth surfaced. When probed about their African-American selection, many admitted that they would be more comfortable doing business with an African-American loan officer. Respondents explained that the African-American loan officer "would best understand their needs, and would not judge them." The exercise was successful at "disarming" these respondents and encouraging them to reveal their true values and beliefs, and disregard politically correct answers.

- **Don't abandon tradition:** We are not advocating abandoning traditional approaches. They have served our clients and the African-American community well over the years. But it is important that marketers and researchers understand that African Americans respond emotionally to their environment, and other situations. In most cases, this is what clients want. However, the outcome of the research and your marketing project may depend on how you approach African Americans and your success in getting them to be more thoughtful respondents.

TEN

The Importance of Race in Marketing

Marketers need to understand that race is not an ugly word.
—Bridgette O'Neal, Executive Director,
Brand Development, *Essence* magazine

In the business and marketing arenas, most of us are still not comfortable talking about race. In fact, some marketers believe that the practice of marketing to consumers based on race is obsolete. As mentioned throughout this book, they assert that other factors, such as lifestyle, are more important, in part because those factors cross racial lines. Race, however, is a powerful means for defining one's culture and experiences. It has also served, throughout history, as a basis on which individuals have been classified, oppressed, protected, and rewarded.

Cora Daniels, author of *Black Power Inc: The New Voice of Success,* which explores what race means to young Black professionals born during the post-civil rights era, interviewed Wishart Edwards, an investment banking partner at the Swiss Bank UBS, in a recent article. Edward attests, "Like it or not, race guides everything we do. Because at the end of the day, you are always going to be a Black person trying to get something that no one wants to give you."[112]

Courtney Counts, Account Director for Guerrilla Tactics Media (GTM), an award winning, experiential-marketing and communications agency, agrees. Despite finding opportunities with multicultural segments where GTM's urban and hip-hop targets are vastly influenced by African-American trends, Counts says "I'm always going to be that Black man in America in terms of (being perceived) as unequal. There is this imbalance in America rooted in an institutional mindset that believes we are second level citizens."[113]

Not acknowledging race or culture in marketing or communications plans does not eliminate African Americans' desire for an emotional connection with these characteristics and customs. Nor does it make race or culture obsolete. Given African Americans' history and general appearance, many believe that they will continue to be easily and visibly identified and judged by race; again more fallout from The Filter. Therefore, marketers need to consider removing their own mirrors and learn to look outside of self and yes, embrace similarities, but begin acknowledging and celebrating the differences.

During a qualitative study for a major automobile manufacturer in 2004 where equal numbers of focus groups and ethnographies were conducted with whites, Latinos, and African Americans, the similarities in attitudinal mindsets between the groups were few, but the differences, especially between African Americans and whites were many. For example, respondents were given an exercise to create a collage about their current lifestyle, dreams, and desires. When each presented their collages, all three segments were in agreement that strong family orientation and traditional values were important. However, the differences were noted in several areas but particularly between African Americans and whites as follows:

- When responding to the question about their future, travel, and how well they fit in with current society, for whites the future was described as full of uncertainty, but most African Americans believed that the future was full of hope, then opportunity.

- Whites indicated that they want to fit in with their community, whereas African Americans want recognition and respect from America. Again, this is consistent with other syndicated studies mentioned earlier about African Americans' need to feel respected by white America.

- African Americans indicated that they were concerned with the success of their children, whereas whites noted that they were concerned with the work ethic of their children.

The results from the study go on to reveal other differences between the segments, but again, the point is twofold: First, many of these differences materialized from racial and cultural situations, and second, just think of the number of opportunities that would be left on the table if marketers were to embrace only the similarities.

> ### How Black and Whites Differ on Race and Civil Rights Today
>
> Some findings from Gallup's *2003 Race Relation Survey* among African American and white respondents aged 18 and older indicated how Blacks and whites differ on issues of race and Civil Rights. For many African Americans the findings support their belief that they are not recognized and treated as equals.
>
> - 72 percent of African Americans believe race will always be a problem vs. 62 percent of whites
> - Only 21 percent of African Americans perceive most Civil Rights goals have been achieved vs. 56 percent of whites
>
> **56% of whites perceive most Civil Rights goals have been met—but only 21% of Blacks agree.**
>
> - 66 percent of African Americans believe the Civil Rights Movement is extremely important to America's future vs. only 23 percent of whites.

"I Didn't Know..."

In 2005, with all the multicultural, multiracial fanfare, it's amazing that so many marketers lack an understanding about who African Americans are, and why they do what they do.

The above are some of the sweetest words to hear from white marketers or researchers when they realize the important connection and often frustrations that many African Americans have with culture and race.

After participating in several meetings with *Essence* magazine staffers and their research consultants learning about cultural insights and frustrations, Freddie Clary of Time, Inc., remarked, "I didn't know." When Ms. Clary was asked to clarify her remark, she explained, "For years, I was a part of big companies that pursued general-market segments. It has been helpful in a personal way, to understand the point of view about Black women. So when a Black woman says to me, 'this is where I'm coming from,' I get it."[114]

In recent focus groups, when African-American women reviewed the finished, on-air Tide-with-Downy TV spot with the Black father and child mentioned earlier (page 50) the "oohs" and "aahs" and "I love that commercial" were blurted from respondents before the commercial ended. One respondent commented, "It's about time they showed a loving Black man with his child," the astonished white clients behind the mirror responded, "I didn't know."

Savoy publisher, Hermene Hartman, was on the money when she said that African Americans are starved for more positive images of themselves. Although African Americans have made and are making great strides, the struggle for equality for most African Americans still continues.

A New America, But Race Still Matters

For many African Americans, there is little badge value in being perceived as white, but there is a new way to be Black. It's a new way for African Americans not to reject the system, but rather to use and celebrate their race and culture for its personal and community goals.

Whether you are an established market leader looking for new markets or a trendy newcomer who thrives on new ideas, the African-American market represents an enormous growth opportunity that can make a major difference in your ability, not only to win, but also to win big in the new, more-diverse 21st century.

In an increasingly tough business environment, the goal is to obtain a "bigger bang" from marketing via campaigns through highly targeted messages. Therefore, marketers who do not intimately understand the different mindset, evolving complexities, cultural influence, and the preference for advertised brands of the African-American market, place their companies at a competitive disadvantage now, and into the future.

With a more in-depth and insightful understanding of the African-American consumer, you can:

- Preempt your competition.
- Unveil new areas of business growth for your company.
- Increase your brand sales.
- Increase your market share.
- Improve your return on marketing resources (ROM).
- More intelligently justify the relative size and allocation of your marketing budgets.

- Enhance your brand image and appeal among other consumer segments that are influenced by what Black people do and say.

- Provide a better gauge for measuring results.

Along the way, we hope we have convinced you to reconsider and or rethink your approach to marketing to the African-American consumer, or that your passion has been rekindled for this pioneer ethnic market segment.

We encourage you to be mindful of the words of Cora Daniels that describe African Americans in a similar way to the *What is Black* poem in the Prologue: "This generation of African Americans is aggressive, focused, impatient, unwavering, bold, and demanding when it comes to race. Black is first; Black is what matters; Black is important, not less.[115]

Glossary

Market Research

The American Institute of Small businesses defines *Market Research* very simply as a way to get particular information from certain people and/or other available resources.

Qualitative Research

- Exploratory and Directional: Answers the "Why" question
- Used to gather detailed opinions from consumers or various publics
- Used to generate dialogue with target and new ideas
- Provides input for advertising, concept development/ refinement
- Provides direction for quantitative studies, (i.e., identify segments/understand and learn consumer language and issues)
- Used as a follow-up to quantitative testing to more fully explore and understand key issues and results
- In general, qualitative research should be treated as exploratory, not evaluative, research. It is a *not* a substitute for quantitative research.
- Ethnographic and Observational Research
  - Direct observation in natural context
  - Often referred to as on-site or at-home studies
  - Intensive face-to-face involvement
  - Closest view of the consumer
  - Highly filtered

- Accounts for cultural division
- Can see other people and their influence in the environment
- Can obtain novel cultural and lifestyle insights
- Observe rituals and routines of produce usage
- Gain an understanding of standards for satisfaction language and words, nicknames, and so forth.

Quantitative Research

- Used for measuring any phenomenon, validating a hypothesis, identifying groups/segments, etc.
- Measurement is central to quantitative research

There are basically two types of measurements made by quantitative research:

- *Facts:* for example, age, sex, race, purchases, income, sales, socio-economic levels
- *Psychographics:* attitudes, beliefs, feelings, usually measured by carefully tested scales.

Account Planning

Account Planning means making sure the "voice of the consumer" is heard in every aspect of the advertising process.

- Hearing the voice of the consumer means understanding the "heart," insights, and nuances of people's lifestyles. Among African Americans, it's understanding the "Black Experience."
- Helps people (marketers/advertisers) understand the relationship between consumers and brands
- Use elements of consumer research
- Use elements of strategic planning

U.S. African-American Profile Summary

2000 Median Household Income	$30,439
Median Age	29.4
Average household size	3.5
Own home	47%
High school diploma (age 25 and older)	79%
Have bachelor's degree	17%
Navigate Internet (home and work)	36%
Reside in South	54%
Religion very important	79%
Spending Power	$723.0 billion

Sources: 2000 Census; Chicago Tribune (6/9/2002), 2002 Hunter-Miller Group Market Snapshot

Top 10 African-American Markets

(Black alone only; not in combination with another race)

Top Ten African-American Markets	Population		
	African American	Total	% African-American
New York, NY	2,129,762	8,008,278	26.6%
Chicago, IL	1,065,009	2,896,016	36.8%
Detroit, MI	775,772	951,270	81.6%
Philadelphia, PA	655,824	1,517,550	43.2%
Houston, TX	494,496	1,953,631	25.3%
Baltimore, MD	418,951	651,154	64.3%
Los Angeles, CA	415,915	3,694,820	11.3%
Memphis, TN	399,208	650,100	61.4%
Washington, DC	343,312	572,059	60.0%
New Orleans, LA	325,947	484,674	67.3%
Total of Top Ten Places	**7,024,196**	**21,379,552**	**32.9%**
Total Population	34,658,190	281,421,906	12.3%
Percent of Total Population in Top Ten Places	20.3%	7.6%	N/A

Source: The Black Population: 2000, Census 2000 Brief, U.S. Census Bureau

African-American Marketing Resource Guide

This is a partial listing of companies that have expertise with the African-American market:

Advertising Agencies

Anderson Communications
2245 Godby Road
Atlanta, GA 30349
T: (404) 766-8000 • F: (404) 767-5264
www.andercom.com
Contact: Al Anderson, President

Burrell Communications Group, L.L.C.
233 North Michigan, Floor 29
Chicago, IL 60601
T: (312) 297-9600 • F: (312) 443-0974
www.burrell.com
Contacts: Fay Ferguson, CEO; McGhee Williams, CEO; Steve Conner, CEO

Danielle Ashley
111 East Wacker Drive
Chicago, IL 60601
T: (312) 240-9900 • F: (312) 240-9901
www.danielleashley.com
Contact: Tracey Alston, President/CEO

Circulation Expertí
707 Westchester Avenue, Suite 309
White Plains, NY 10604
T: (914) 948-8144 • F: (914) 948-1332
www.experti.com
Contact: W. Garrison Jackson, President/CEO

Compas Inc.
Woodland Falls Corporate Park
220 Lake Drive East, Suite 102
Cherry Hill, NJ 08002
T: (856) 667-8577 • F: (856) 667-8430
www.compasonline.com
Contact: Stan Woodland, CEO

Crawley Haskins & Rodgers
Public Relations & Advertising
Penn Mutual Towers
510 Walnut Street, Suite 1300
Philadelphia, PA 19106
T: (215) 922-7184 • F: (215) 922-7189
Contact: A. Bruce Crawley

R.J. Dale Advertising
211 E. Ontario Street, Suite 200
Chicago, IL 60611
T: (312) 644-2316 • F: (312) 644-2688
www.rjdale.com
Contact: Robert Dale, President/CEO

Equals Three Communications, Inc.
7910 Woodmont Avenue, Suite 200
Bethesda, MD 10814-3015
T: (310) 652-5264 • F: (301) 652-5264
www.equals3.com
Contact: Eugene M. Faison, Jr., CEO

Footsteps Group
200 Varick Street, Suite 610
New York, NY 10014
T: (212) 924-6432 • F: (212) 924-5669
www.footstepsgroup.net
Contact: Verdia Johnson, President

Fuse, Inc.
1409 Washington Avenue
Saint Louis, MO 63013
T: (314) 421-4040 • F: (314) 421-3033
www.fuseadvertising.com
Contact: Clifford Franklin, President

Global Hue
26555 Evergreen, Suite 1700
Southfield, MI 48076
T: (248) 223-8900 • F: (248) 304-5960
www.globalhue.com
Contact: Donald A. Coleman, CEO

Guerrilla Tactics Marketing & Media
256 Walker Street, Suite 100
Atlanta, GA 30313
T: (404) 522-0486 • F: (404) 522-2486
www.gtmcentral.com
Contacts: Karl Carter, Partner;
Davis Evans, Partner; Shawn Howard,
Partner; Courntey Counts, Partner;
Kimbo Tom, Partner

Images USA
914 Howell Mill Road, NW
Atlanta, GA 30318
T: (404) 892-2931 • F: (404) 892-8651
www.imagesusa.net
Contact: Robert L. McNeil, Jr., CEO

Intersect Urban
21 East Huron, Suite 3505
Chicago, IL 60611
T: (312) 961-6136
www.intersecturban.com
Contact: Phillip M. Gant III

LaGrant Communications
555 South Flower Street, Suite 700
Los Angeles, CA 90071
T: (323) 469-8680 • F: (323) 469-8683
www.lagrant.com
Contact: Kim L. Hunter, President/CEO

Matlock Advertising &
Public Relations
1545 Peachtree Street N.E., Suite 300
Atlanta, GA 30309
T: (404) 872-3200 • F: (404) 876-4929
www.matlock-adpr.com
Contact: Kent Matlock, President

E. Morris Communications
820 North Orleans
Chicago, IL 60610
T: (312) 943-2900 • F: (312) 943-5856
www.emorris.com
Contact: Eugene Morris, CEO

Muse Cordero Chen & Partners
6100 Wilshire Boulevard
Los Angeles, CA 90048
T: (323) 954-1655 • F: (323) 954-9260
www.musecordero.com
Contact: Jo Muse, Chairman/CEO/
Creative Director

Prime Access, Inc.
345 Seventh Avenue
New York, NY 10001
T: (212) 868-6800 • F: (212) 868-9495

www.primeaccess.net
Contact: Howard Buford, President/CEO

Spike DDB
437 Madison Avenue
New York, NY 10022
www.spikeddb.com
T: (212) 415-3100 • F: (212) 415-3101
Contact: Dana Wade, President

SWG&M
720 Brazos, Suite 300
Austin, TX 78701
T: (512) 476-7949 • F: (512) 476-7950
www.swgm.com
Contact: Bob Wingo, President/CEO

Sykes Communications, Inc.
1800 West Loop S, Suite 1130
Houston, TX 77027
T: (713) 223-0333 • F: (713) 223-0496
www.sykescommunications.com
Contact: Ray Sykes, CEO

Tapestry, *multicultural division of*
Starcom Media Vest Group
35 West Wacker Drive
Chicago, IL 60601
T: (312) 220-6262 • F: (312) 220-6561
www.tapestrypartners.com
Contact: Monica Gadsby, CEO

True Agency
5353 Grosvenor Boulevard
Los Angeles, CA 90066
T: (310) 305-5250 • F: (310) 305-6215
www.true310.com
Contact: Valencia Gayles, COO

UniWorld Group, Inc.
110 Avenue of the Americas
New York, NY 10013
T: (212) 219-1600 • F: (212) 219-6395
www.uniworldgroup.com
Contact: Byron E. Lewis, Sr., CEO

Vanguard Communications
100 Ryders Lane, Suite 139
Milltown, NJ 08850
T: (732) 238-7782 • F: (732) 257-2131
www.vanguardcomm.com
Contact: Esther Novak, President

Vigilante
41 Madison Avenue, 41st Floor
New York, NY 10010
T: (212) 545-2850 • F: (212) 545-2855
www.vigilantenyc.com
Contact: Larry Woodward, CEO

Webb Patterson Communications
12 West Parrish Street
Durham, NC 27701
T: (919) 680-6111 • F: (919) 680-6141
www.webbpatterson.com
Contact: Carl Webb, President/CEO

The Wimbley Group, Inc.
2550 West Golf Road
Rolling Meadows, IL 60008
T: (630) 775-7500 • F: (630) 290-1322
www.wimbleygroup.com
Contact: Charles L. Wimbley, Sr.

Carol H. Williams Advertising
555 12th Street, Suite 1700
Oakland, CA 94607
T: (510) 763-5200
875 North Michigan
Chicago, IL 60611
T: (312) 836-7919
www.carolhwilliams.com
Contact: Carol H. Williams, President

Market Research Companies

A+ Marketing Research (Recruiting)
7040 South Prairie Avenue
Chicago, IL 60637
T: (773) 651-3115 • F: (773) 651-4569
rrcmarlon@yahoo.com
Contact: Marion Batey, President

Kathryn Alexander Enterprises, Inc.
215 West 95th Street, Suite 14L
New York, NY 10025
T: (212) 222-0216 • F: (212) 222-0528
Contact: Kathryn Alexander

Allen and Partners, Inc.
620 Sheridan Avenue
Plainfield, NJ 07060
T: (908) 561-4062 • F: (908) 561-6827
www.allenandpartners.com
Contact: Clyde Allen, President

Campbell Communications
140 Debs Place, 17th Floor
New York, NY 10475
T: (718) 671-6989 • F: (718) 671-0359
www.campbell-communications.com
Contact: Ron Campbell, President

CR Market Surveys
Universal City Offices
9510 South Constance Ave., Suite C-6
Chicago, IL 60617
T: (800) 882-1983 • F: (773) 933-0558
www.crmarketsurveys.com
Contact: Cherlyn Robinson, President

M. Davis & Company
1520 Locust Street, Suite 12
Philadelphia, PA 19104
T: (215) 790-8900 • F: (215) 790-8930
www.mdavisco.com
Contact: Morris Davis, President

Ebony Marketing Research, Inc.
2100 Bartow Avenue, Suite 243
New York, NY 10475
T: (718) 320-3220 • F: (718) 320-3996
www.ebonymktg.com
Contact: Ebony Kirkland, President/CEO

Erlich Transcultural Consultants
11430 Burbank Boulevard
North Hollywood, CA 91601
T: (818) 623-2425 • F: (818) 623-2429
www.etcethnic.com
Contact: Andrew Erlich, Ph.D.

Head First Market Research
332 Osprey Point
Stone Mountain, GA 30087
T: (770) 879-5100 • F: (770) 879-0014
www.headfirstinc.com
Contact: Greg Head, President

The Hunter-Miller Group
1525 East 53rd Street, Suite 605
Chicago, IL 60615
T: (773) 363-7420 • F: (773) 363-1415
www.huntermillergroup.com
Contact: Pepper Miller, President

Images Market Research

914 Howell Mill Road, Suite 300
Atlanta, GA 30318
T: (404) 892-2931 • F: (404) 892-8651
www.imagesmarketresearch.net
Contact: Alethia Barry

Michael Johns

1430 Atwood Road
Silver Springs, MD 20906
T: (301) 460-4411 • F: (301) 460-4466
mikjohns@aol.com
Contact: Michael Johns

Johnson & Associates Marketing, Inc.

8011 South Prairie Avenue
Chicago, IL 60619
T: (312) 567-0700
Contact: Debra Johnson-Hall, President

JRH Marketing Services, Inc.

29-27 41st Avenue
New York, NY 11101
T: (718) 786-9640 • F: (718) 786-9642
Contact: Bob Harris, President

The K Group

37 Cranbury Road
Norwalk, CT 06851
T: (203) 849-8400 • F: (203) 849-3230
Contact: Kevin Knight, President

King-Harris Marketing

4610 North 188th Street
Country Club Hills, IL 60478
T: (708) 799-8544
E: dlking1@aol.com
Contact: Debbie King, CEO

New American Dimensions

6955 La Tijera Blvd., Suite B
Los Angeles, CA 90045
T: (310) 670-7835 • F: (310) 670-7158
www.newamericandimensions.com
Contact: Susanna Whitmore, Sr. VP Business Development

NIA Online

23 West Hubbard, Suite 200
Chicago, IL 60610
T: (312) 222-0943 • F: (312) 222-0944
www.niaenterprises.com
Contact: Cheryl Mayberry McKissak, Chairman & CEO

Portico Research

6426 South Kenwood #2S
Chicago, IL 60637
T: (773) 684-6044
www.porticoresearch.com
Contact: Patricia Raspberry, Ph.D. Director of Urban Insights

Precious Issues Research

(Recruiting)
1677 Trapet Avenue
Hazel Crest, IL 60429
T: (708) 474-7122 • F: (708) 474-7129
E: roseprecious@sbcglobal.net
Contact: Rose Ann McLaurin, CEO

Research Explorers

111 New Trier Court
Wilmette, IL 60091
T: (847) 853-0237 • F: (847) 853-1063
www.researchexplorers.com
Contact: Lisa McDonald, President

Riva Market Research

1700 Rockville Pike, Suite 260
Rockville, MD 20852
T: (301) 770-6456 • F: (301) 770-5879
www.rivainc.com
Contact: Naomi Henderson, CEO; Amber Tedesco, VP

Resources Plus

1448 East 52nd Street
Chicago, IL 60615
T: (773) 667-7710
www.resourcesplus.com
Contact: John Porter

V & L Research & Consulting, Inc.

1901 Montreal Rd., Suite 115
Atlanta, GA 30084
T: (770) 908-0003
Contact: Dydra Virgil, President

Research Companies with Syndicated Research Expertise

Arbitron
142 West 57th Street
New York, NY 10019-3300
T: (212) 887-1300
www.arbitron.com

Media Mark Research, Inc.
75 Ninth Avenue, 5th Floor
New York, NY 10011
T: (212) 884-9200 • F: (212) 884-9339
www.mediamark.com

Nielsen Media Research
770 Broadway
New York, NY 10003
T: (646) 654-8300 • F: (646) 654-8990
www.nielsen.com

Scarborough Research
770 Broadway
New York, NY 10003
T: (646) 654-8400 • F: (646) 654-8450
www.scarborough.com

Simmons Market Research Bureau
230 Park Avenue South, 3rd Floor
New York, NY 10003-1566
T: (212) 598-5400 • F: (212) 598-5401
www.simmonsmarketresearch
bureau.com

Yankelovich Partners, Inc.
400 Meadowmont Village Circle,
Suite 431
Chapel Hill, NC 27517
T: (919) 932-8600 • F: (919) 932-8829
www.yankelovich.com

African-American Marketing & Consulting

Allen and Partners, Inc.
620 Sheridan Avenue
Plainfield, NJ 07060
T: (908) 561-4062 • F: (908) 561-6827
www.allenandpartners.com
Contact: Clyde Allen, President

Chatham Consulting Group
P.O. Box 43-6821 (Station H)
Chicago, IL 60643
T: (773) 374-6936
www.chathamchicago.com
Contact: Michael Bolden, CEO

Herb Kemp
What's Black About It?
6 Arrowhead Road
Westport, CT 06880
T: (203) 255-4105 • F: (203) 319-1988
E: hkemp@optonline.net

Lundy Marketing Group
P.O. Box 703736
Dallas, TX 75370
T: 972-377-9026 • F: 972-377-9031
Contact: Larry Lundy, President

The 85% Niche, LLC
*Rallying the Power of Women for
Exponential Business Results*
286 Moran Road
Grosse Pointe Farms, MI 48236

T: (313) 885-5220 • F: (313) 885-5633
www.85percentniche.com
MMuley@85percentniche.com
Miriam Muléy, Founder & CEO

The MOBE Marketing Institute
7425 South Michigan Avenue
Chicago, IL 60619
T: (773) 651-8008 • F: (773) 651-8018
www.mobe.com
Contact: Yvette Moyo; Rael Jackson

The Rebel Organization
6300 Wilshire Boulevard, Suite 1750
Los Angeles, CA 90048
T: (323) 315-1704 • F: (323) 784-7900
www.Rebelorganization.com
Contact: Jeff Meade, Business Development Manager

SMSi
Segmented Marketing Services
4265 Brownsboro Road, Suite 225
Winston-Salem, NC 27106-3425
T: (336) 759-7477 • F: (336) 759-7212
www.segmentedmarketing.com
Contact: Lafayette Jones / Sandra Miller-Jones

The Triad Communications
6709 La Tuera Blvd., Suite 399
Los Angeles, CA 90045
T: (310) 854-8890 • F: (310) 417-3481
E: triadla@aol.com
Contact: Yvette Richardson-Hudson, VP

Zebra Strategies
2565 Broadway, Suite 393
New York, NY 10025
T: (212) 860-7128 • F: (917) 591-2934
www.zstrategies.net
Contact: Denene Jonielle, President

PR Agencies & Media Companies

Beaman Media & PR
737 North Michigan Avenue
Chicago, IL 60611
T: (312) 751-9689 • F: (312) 751-9405
www.beamaninc.com
Contact: Robin Beaman, President

The Marketing Store, Inc.
7901 Fayette Street, 1st Floor
Philadelphia, PA 19150
T: (215) 924-6263
E: MARKETSTOR@aol.com
Contact: Bruce B. Rush, President

DJC Communications
1326 East 48th Street
Chicago, IL 60615
T: (773) 548-7642
www.djcinc.com
Contact: Deborah J. Crable, President

Melody's Service
9406 South St. Lawrence
Chicago, IL 60619
T: (773) 660-2001
Contact: Melody McDowell

Kensey + Kensy Communications
5212 South Dorchester Avenue
Chicago, IL 60615
T: (773) 288-8776
Contact: Barbara Kensy, President

Public Image Relations, Inc.
30 East Elm Street, Suite 3A
Chicago, IL 60611
www.publicrelations.com
Contact: B. J. Parker, President

African-American Leading Media

Magazines

African-American Medical Network
6601 Center Drive West, Suite 521
Los Angeles, CA 90045
T: (301) 348-8170 • F: (301) 348-8171
www.africanamericannetwork.com
Contact: Charles Richardson, President

Drug Store News
425 Park Avenue
New York, NY 10022
T: (800) 766-6999
www.drugstorenews.com

Ebony / Jet Magazines
820 South Michigan Avenue
Chicago, IL 60605
T: (312) 322-9200
www.ebonymag.com
Contact: Linda Johnson, CEO

African-American Golfers Digest
139 Fulton Street, Suite 209
New York, NY 10038
T: (212) 571-6559
www.africanamericangolfers.com
Contact: Debert Cook, Publisher

Black Enterprise
130 Fifth Avenue, 10th Floor
New York, NY 10011-43999
T: (212) 242-8000
Contact: Earl Graves, Jr., CEO

Essence Communications Partners
1500 Broadway, 6th Floor
New York, NY 10036
T: (212) 642-0600 • F: (212) 921-5173
www.essence.com
Contact: Michelle Ebanks, President

Hype Hair
210 Route 4 East, Suite 211
Paramus, NJ 07652-5103
T: (201) 843-4004
Contact: Adrienne Moore, Editor

Homes of Color
12138 Central Avenue #303
Mitchellville, MO 20721
T: (301) 352-7690
www.homesofcolor.net
Contacts: John & Corece Gwynn,
Publishers

Pathfinders Magazine
6325 Germantown Avenue
Philadelphia, PA 19144
T: (215) 438-2140 • F: (215) 438-2144
www.pathfinderstravel.com

Savoy Magazine + N'Digo Profiles
19 North Sangamon
Chicago, IL 60607
T: (312) 822-0202
Contact: Hermene Hartman, Publisher

Savoy Professional
632 Broadway, 7th Floor
New York, NY 10012
T: (212) 352-0840 • F: (212) 352-9282
Contact: Jungle Media Groups:
Sean McDuffy, Jonathan McBride,
Jon Housman, Founders

Sister 2 Sister
P.O. Box 41148
Washington, DC 20018
www.s2smag.com
Contact: Jamie Foster Brown, Publisher

Sophisticate's Black Hair
John Hancock Center
875 North Michigan Ave., Suite 3434
Chicago, IL 60611
T: (312) 266-8680
www.associatedpub.com

The Source
28 West 23rd Street, 10th Floor
New York, NY 10010
T: (212) 253-3700 • F: (212) 253-9344
www.thesource.com

Target Market News Online
228 South Wabash, Suite 210
Chicago, IL 60604
T: (312) 408-1881 • F: (312) 408-1867
www.targetmarketnews.com
Contact: Ken Smikle, President

Upscale Magazine
600 Bronner Brothers Way SW
Atlanta, GA 30310
T: (404) 758-7467
www.upscalemagazine.com

Urban Call
4265 Brownboro Road, Suite 225
Winston-Salem, NC 27106-3425
T: (336) 759-7477 • F: (336) 759-7212
www.urbancall.com
Contact: Lafayette Jones, Sandra Miller-Jones

Vibe Magazine
215 Lexington Avenue
New York, NY 10016
T: (212) 448-7300 • F: (212) 448-7400
www.vibe.com

XXL Magazine
www.xxlmag.com

Cable TV

Black Family TV Channel
www.mbcnetwork.com

TV One
1010 Wayne Avenue, 10th Floor
Silver Spring, MD 20910
T: (301) 755-0400
www.TV-one.tv
Contact: Johnathan Rodgers, CEO

Showtime
Showtime Network, Inc.
1633 Broadway
New York, NY 10019
www.sho.com

HBO
1100 Avenue of the Americas
New York, NY 10036-6712
T: (212) 512-1000
www.hbo.com
Contact: Chris Albrecht, Chairman & CEO

Radio

American Urban Radio Networks
655 3RD Avenue
New York, NY 10017
T: (212) 883-2100
www.aurnol.com
Contact: Howard Eisen, V.P Sales

Clear Channel
200 Basse Road
San Antonio, TX 78209
T: (210) 822-2828
www.clearchannel.com

Interep Radio
100 Park Avenue, 5th & 6th Floors
New York, NY 10017
T: (212) 916-0700 • F: (212) 916-0792
www.interep.com
Contact: Ralph C. Guild, CEO

Katz Media Corporation
125 West 55th Street
New York, NY 10019-5366
T: (212) 424-6000
www.katz-media.com
Contact: Brian Knox, SVP & Director of
Corporate Diversity

Radio One, Inc.
5900 Princess Garden Pkwy, 7th Floor
Landham, MD 20706
T: (301) 306-1111
www.radio-one.com
Contact: Cathy Hughes, Founder/
Albert Hughes, CEO

Motivational and Public Speakers

Shanita B. Akintonde
Creative Notions Group
408 West Winneconna Pkwy. Suite 400
Chicago, IL 60620
T: (773) 224-0320 • F: (773) 224-0615
Shanita_Akintonde@yahoo.com,
shanitaspeaks@yahoo.com

Verdia Barnett-Johnson
7002 Boulevard East, Suite 8-1
Guttenberg, NJ 07093
T: (201) 854-7205
E: verdia714@yahoo.com

Kelvin Boston
Boston Media, LLC
P.O. Box 38571
Baltimore, MD 21231
T: (410) 576-9199
www.moneywise.tv

Contact: keboston@aol.com

Les Brown
P.O. Box 27380
Detroit, MI 48227
T: (800) 733-4226 • F: (313) 653-4121
www.lesbrown.com

Stedman Graham
www.StedmanGraham.com
T: (312) 755-0234
Contact: LeVette Straughter (LStraugh-
ter@StedmanGraham.com)

Sporty King
R. King & Associates
7620 West Madison
Forest Park, IL 60130
T: (708) 366-1445 • F: (708) 366-1449
www.sportyking.com

Popular African-American Websites

www.aagamer.com Gaming website that focuses on African-American consumers and
provides game reviews, editorials, polls and forums.

www.africanamericangolfersdigest.com Promotes golf and highlights profiles of
Black golfers across the country.

www.bet.com Home page and multiple links for Black Entertainment TV.

www.blackvoices.com African-American and Black culture community; links for
news, sports, education, work and money, lifestyle, entertainment, and connect.

www.blackwebportal.com Black search engine with yellow pages, websites,
classified, events, news, etc.

www.blackenterprise.com Online companion to *Black Enterprise* magazine, the authority on business and wealth building for African-American consumers.

www.blackplanet.com The largest African-American website; links for online communities for ethnic audiences and career opportunities.

www.blackamericaweb.com Links for news, leisure and fun, Tom Joyner Foundation, praise and inspiration, health, career and finances.

www.blackfind.com Search engine; thousands of Black websites and businesses.

www.black-collegian.com Career site for students of color; jobs, employer profiles, awards, graduate school opportunities, career and industry reports.

www.blackworld.com Internet U.S. and worldwide directory for money and finance, entertainment, travel, jobs, and top stories targeting people of color.

www.blacksinglesconnection.com Singles online source for creating relationships; photo gallery, chat rooms, message boards, etc.

www.diversityinc.com Online news magazine; provides education and clarity on the business benefits of diversity. Also features links to book store, career center, resource guide, and forum.

www.essence.com Online companion to *Essence* magazine, the authority on African-American women; contains articles, events, online panel.

www.ebony.com Online companion to *Ebony* magazine.

www.huntermillergroup.com Website for author Pepper Miller's research firm; The Black consumer market authority. Includes the Hunter-Miller Market Snapshot—a free electronic bulletin focused on African-American consumers; each issue examines one topic in detail and includes both demographic and psychographic information. Snapshot link covers previous issues dating back to 2002.

www.netweed.com (Hip Hop Press) An online space with a liberal perspective and artsy tendencies; links to a web directory and special projects.

www.mobe.com (Marketing Opportunities in Business and Entertainment) Provides information about its highly sought after African-American business and marketing conferences

www.prohiphop.com Hip-hop blog and business news; multiple links.

www.realmencook.com Information about the leading urban Father's Day event and other Real Men Cook charity programs and events nationwide.

www.targetmarketnews.com Free online news magazine; Includes Black consumer and market statistics and the latest industry news when it happens.

www.urbankind.com Wireless hip-hop and urban lifestyle; mobile channel and community guide.

www.urbanmecca.com Information about urban culture, lifestyle and news; articles and website directory; general interest site catering to African Americans.

www.tnj.com (The Network Journal) Online magazine dedicated to educating and empowering Black professionals and small business owners.

www.vibe.com Online urban authority; caters to youth market and tech-savvy music enthusiasts.

Notes

1. "The Multicultural Economy 2004, America's Minority Buying Power" by Jeffery M. Humphreys, Selig Center for Economic Growth, University of Georgia, Third Quarter 2004.
2. "Marketing Missing Mark: Blacks Largely Ignored," by M. Price, *New York Daily News*, January 17, 2005.
3. "Multiracial Scenes Now Common in Ads," *DiversityInc.com*, February 18, 2005.
4. "Colorblind Marketing: Progress or Peril?" by Angela Johnson, *DiversityInc.com*, June 14, 2004.
5. "Marketers' New Rule: No Longer About Race for African Americans," by Valerie Seckler, *Women's Wear Daily*, March 27, 2002.
6. *Ibid.*
7. "BIASED! What Standardized Tests Cost Corporate America," *Diversity Inc.* magazine, April/May 2004.
8. Personal Interview with Dr. Jeremiah A. Wright, Jr., March 2005.
9. "African Americans Aren't Dark-Skinned Whites" C. S. Brown, *DiversityInc.com*, December 6, 2004.
10. *Ibid.*
11. "Marketers' New Rule: No Longer About Race for African Americans," by Valerie Seckler, *Women's Wear Daily*, March 27, 2002.
12. "Who's That Girl: Television's Role in the Body Image Development of Young White and Black Women," by L. M. Ward, et. Al., University of Michigan.
13. African-American Market Profile, Magazine Publishers of America, 2004
14. "Study finds black travelers more likely than other groups to shop during travel," *Targetmarketnews.com*, January 16, 2004.
15. 2004 Ariel Capital Management/Charles Schwab Black Investor Survey.
16. *Black Power, Inc: The New Voice of Success*, by Cora Daniels, J. Wiley & Sons, 2004.
17. *American Skin Pop Culture, Big Business, & The End Of White America*, by Leon E. Wynter, Crown, August 2002.
18. "Respecting the Black Experience: 'Urban' Misses Mark, Uniworld Leader Says," by Linda Bean, *DiversityInc.com*, July 08, 2003.
19. "Ched-da urban apparel brand to test-launch in Northeast," by Mike Duff, *Drug Store News Retailing Today*, September 9, 2002.
20. Yankelovich African-American Monitor, 2001.
21. *Ibid.*
22. "All-Star Super Bowl Ads on the Way," by Holly M. Sanders, *New York Post*, January 30, 2005.
23. *American Behind the Colorline*, by Henry Louis Gates Jr., Warner Books, 2004.
24. Personal interview with Rev. Dr. Jeremiah A. Wright, Jr., Sr., Pastor, Trinity United Church of Christ, Chicago, IL.
25. Personal interview with Jill Nelson, award winning author of *Volunteer Slavery, Straight, No Chaser, Police Brutality,* and *Sexual Healing.*

26. Personal Interview with Darius Howard of GMT Marketing.
27. *Yankelovich African-American Monitor*, 1995; *Burrell Yankelovich Multicultural Monitor*, 2005
28. "Does Cosby Help?" by Ellis Cose, *Newsweek*, December 27, 2004.
29. *Marketing and Consumer Identity in Multicultural America*, Marye C. Tharp, Sage Publications, 2001.
30. "Natalie Portman Apologizes for Black Quote," *DiversityInc.com* December 9, 2004.
31. "Ad Gaffe" *Fast Company*, May 2005.
32. "Marketers' New Rule: No Longer About Race for African Americans," by V. Seckler, *Women's Wear Daily*, March 27, 2002.
33. 2003 Yankelovich Monitor, Multicultural Market Study in collaboration with Cheskin and Images USA.
34. "Marketers' New Rule: No Longer About Race for African Americans," by V. Seckler, *Women's Wear Daily*, March 27, 2002.
35. Yankelovich, *Multicultural Monitor*, 2003.
36. "A Risque Ad on the Bus, If you Speak Hip-Hop," by Anthony Ramirez, *The New York Times*, November 6, 2004
37. "Akademiks Ads Pulled in New York," by Clove Hope, in *ALLHIPHOP NEWS*, November 5, 2004.
38. *The Hilltop*, The Student Voice of Howard University, December 3, 2004.
39. "Unstoppable: A Conversation with Melvin Van Peebles, Gordon Parks & Ossie Davis," Black Starz Cable Network, February 13, 2005.
40. *America Behind the Colorline*, by Henry Louis Gates, Jr., New York: Warner Books, 2004.
41. *Black Power, Inc: The New Voice of Success*, by Cora Daniels, J. Wiley & Sons, 2004.
42. *America Behind the Color Line*, Henry Louis Gates, Jr. Warner Books, 2004
43. HBO Usher Live in Concert, TV program
44. "The Black Teen Explosion," *Ebony*, April 2004.
45. "The New Marketing Realm: Hip-Hop's Urban Mindset Crosses All Demographics," By Yoji Cole, *Diversity Inc.com*, August 22, 2003.
46. *Ibid.*
47. "Cornrows: Style and Substance," *Africana.com*, January 29, 2004.
48. "Ethnic Teens Drive the Market" by Lafayette Jones, *The U.S. Tweens Market*, February 1, 2001.
49. *Ibid.*
50. "The New Marketing Realm: Hip-Hop's Urban Mindset Crosses All Demographics," by Yoji Cole, *Diversity Inc.com*, August 22, 2003.
51. "The Black Teen Explosion," *Ebony*, April 2004.
52. *The U.S. Tweens Market*, Packaged Facts, February 1, 2001.
53. *Ibid.*
54. *Ibid.*
55. *Ibid.*
56. "Teen TV and Lil Romeo hits Orlando with his P. Miller Baller's Basketball Team," *RnB*, August 3, 2004.
57. U.S. Census Bureau, 2002
58. *Ibid.*
59. "African-American and Latino kids, less likely to receive an allowance," *Marketing to Emerging Minorities*, October 2002.

60. Hunter-Miller Group Market Snapshot, *Tweens: Market Savvy with Money to Spend*, (An Update) December 2004.

61. "African-American Children Hard-Hit by Alcopop Ads," National Association of African Americans for Positive Imagery, July 18, 2002.

62. "Family Life and School Experience: Factors in the Racial Identity Development of Black Youth in White Communities," by Beverly Daniel Tatum, *Journal of Social Issues*, Spring 2004.

63. "Marketers' New Rule: No Longer About Race for African Americans," Valerie Seckler, *Women's Wear Daily*, March 27, 2002.

64. *Ibid.*

65. *Women of Color Are on a Buying Spree, DiversityInc.com*, July 1, 2004; The Hunter-Miller Group Market Snapshot, June 27, 2004.

66. PR Newswire, January 19, 2004.

67. "African-American Women Gaining in Biz Starts," by Sheryl Nance-Nash, We News, February 13, 2005.

68. "Black Women Ignore Many of Media's Beauty Ideals," by Dakota Smith, *Women's eNews*, December 27, 2004.

69. *Ibid.*

70. "Who's That Girl?: Television's Role in the Body Image Development of Young White and Black Women," by L.M. Ward, et. al. University of Michigan.

71. *Slim Down Sister: The African-American Woman's Guide to Healthy, Permanent Weight Loss*, by Roniece Weaver, Fabiola Gaines, and Angela Ebron, Plume Books, 2001.

72. *I Left My Backdoor Open*, by April Sinclair, Hyperion Publishers, 1999, p. 2.

73. "Beauty's Got Back," *DiversityInc.com* , September 1, 2004

74. *Ibid.*

75. "Will Curvier Mannequins Bring Big Booty to the Fashion Industry?" *DiversityInc.com*, December 13, 2004.

76. "Mass Media Damaging African-American Women's Body Esteem," a news release about a study conducted by Cynthia Frisby at the Missouri University School of Journalism, later published in *Journal of Black Studies*, March 2004, *http://journalism.missouri.edu/news/releases/2003/2003-09-08-frisby.html*.

77. 2005 *Window on Our Women II*, Essence Communications.

78. "Color Bind," by Sandra Yin, *American Demographics*, September 1, 2003.

79. "Smooth Operations," by Allison Samuels with Mary Carmicheal, *Newsweek*, July 5, 2004.

80. "African-American Women Read More Magazines," *www.Diversity Inc.com*, Factoids, September 9, 2004.

81. U.S. Census Bureau, 2000 and 2002.

82. 1995 Yankelovich *African American Monitor;* 2003 Yankelovich *Monitor Multicultural Marketing Study.*

83. McGhee Williams, Partner, Burrell Communications, Inc.

84. *What is Cool? Understanding Black Manhood in America* by Marlene Kim Connor, Agate Publishing, 2003.

85. The Hunter-Miller Group qualitative research, 2004.

86. "Is the Media Still Whitewashed?" by Angela Johnson-Meadows, *DiversityInc.com*, January 13, 2005.

87. "Diversity in Ads Not Reflected in Real Life," by Associated Press, February 22, 1005, *St. Petersburg Times Online, www.sptimes.com*.

88. "McDonald's Launches Year Long Celebration of African American History," Press Release, McDonald's USA, January 31, 2002 Press Release *http://www.mcdonalds.com/usa/news/current/conpr01312002c.html.*

89. "Black History and Ads Don't Mix, Activists Say," A. Thomas-Lester, *www. WashingtonPost.com*, February 24, 2005.

90. DePaul University Study, by Dr. Robert Pitts, 1990.

91. Sam Chisholm, CEO, Chisholm Mingo Group.

92. "As the Melting Pot Simmers, Ethnic Media Reaches People of Color," by Kipp Cheng, *DiversityInc.com*, April 24, 2004.

93. Don Coleman *Yankelovich Monitor*, 2000.

94. "Marketing Missing Mark: Blacks Largely Ignored," by M. Price, *New York Daily News*, January 17, 2005.

95. National Association of Minority Media Executives News, February 2001.

96. Personal Interview with Darius Evans, March 2005.

97. Arbitron's *Black Radio Today*, 2005 Edition.

98. Personal interview with Brad Sanders, May 2005.

99. "One More Choice," by Megan Larson, *Mediaweek*, April 4, 2005.

100. Dimensions Quarterly Newsletter, First Quarter 2005, *New American Dimensions*, *www.newamericandimensions.com.*

101. "One More Choice," by Megan Larson, *Mediaweek*, April 4, 2005

102. *Ibid.*

103. *African-American Market Profile*, Magazine Publishers of America, 2004.

104. Nielsen/Net Ratings, 2004

105. Pew Internet and American Life Project, 2004

106. Digital Marketing Services, 2004

107. "Try It You'll Like It Reaching Ethnic Consumers With Free Product Samples," by Lafayette Jones, *Exposé Household Products 2003,* Vol. 6, Issue 5, an official publication of the Efficient Promotion Planning Session conferences.

108. "The Vanishing Mass Market," by Anthony Blanco, *Business Week*, July 12, 2004.

109. 2004 ANA *Multicultural Marketing Survey*.

110. U.S. Census Bureau, 2000,

111. Keynote Speech at the 49th Annual Advertising Research Foundation Convention, April 10, 2003.

112. "Young, Gifted, Black—And Out of Here," by Cora Daniels, *Fortune Magazine*, May 3, 2004.

113. *Ibid.*

114. Personal interview with Freddie Clary, March 2005.

115. *Power, Inc.: The New Voice of Success*, Cora Daniels, J. Wiley & Sons, 2004.

Index

About the Authors

Pepper Miller and Herb Kemp are passionate advocates of helping twenty-first century marketers understand the absolute and relative value of the African-American consumer market as a major growth opportunity in a global society.

Since their careers first intersected in the early 1980s when they met in the Chicago offices of J. Walter Thompson, they have had the opportunity to work together as colleagues and partners targeting African-American consumers for America's leading Fortune 500 companies. The lessons learned through more than 25 years of experience are the basis for *What's Black About It?* The book is a catalog of key insights derived from observations of African-American attitudes, behaviors and opinions, by the authors and other authorities on the subject.

In 1985, Pepper founded The Hunter-Miller Group (HMG), a Chicago-based consumer-research, trend-analysis, and marketing-strategy company. The business is dedicated to helping Fortune 500 companies understand how to market their products and messages to the African-American consumer. These clients include: American Airlines, Allstate, General Motors, GlaxoSmithKline, Hallmark, Neutrogena, State Farm, Wells Fargo, Denny's, and Texaco, as well as not-for-profit organizations such as the Chicago Symphony Orchestra, and the Chicago Housing Authority. HMG's services are sought by advertising agencies, including Young & Rubicam, BBDO, Burrell

Communications, Footsteps, Spike DDB, Carol H. Williams, and the
Uniworld Group.

Because few African Americans are aware of career opportunities in
market research, Pepper established the Ruth C. Hunter Market
Research Scholarship Fund with Chicago's N'Digo Foundation to
expose and encourage African-American high school students to consider market research as a career option.

HMG also publishes *Market Snapshot,* a free monthly statistical electronic bulletin focused on African-American consumers.

Herb (the talking brain) is one of the brightest multicultural
marketing-and-advertising experts in the country, with more than 20
years of experience targeting African-American consumers for some
of America's Fortune 500 companies, including Burger King, General
Motors, Kodak, the U.S. Army, Denny's, Texaco, Anheuser-Busch, Seagram's, Toys "R" Us, and AT&T.

He has worked on the client side in decision-making general marketing positions at Pfizer, General Foods, and Chesebrough-Ponds,
transitioning to senior-level general-market advertising-agency responsibility at J. Walter Thompson and Ogilvy and Mather. More recently,
Herb served as President, and as Executive VP at two of the largest
African-American ad agencies, the Uniworld Group and the Chisholm
Mingo Group, respectively.

Today, Herb is the founder of What's Black About It, a Westport,
Connecticut–based marketing consultancy dedicated to providing the
cultural insights and strategic planning tools essential to building business with African-American consumers.